ASSERTIVENESS

Standing Up for Yourself and Learning How to Say No

(Assertiveness & Self-esteem and Effective Modern Communication Skills)

Barbara Council

Published by Darby Connor

Barbara Council

All Rights Reserved

Assertiveness: Standing Up for Yourself and Learning How to Say No (Assertiveness & Self-esteem and Effective Modern Communication Skills)

ISBN 978-1-77485-372-6

All rights reserved. No part of this guide may be reproduced in any form without permission in writing from the publisher except in the case of brief quotations embodied in critical articles or reviews.

Legal & Disclaimer

The information contained in this book is not designed to replace or take the place of any form of medicine or professional medical advice. The information in this book has been provided for educational and entertainment purposes only.

The information contained in this book has been compiled from sources deemed reliable, and it is accurate to the best of the Author's knowledge; however, the Author cannot guarantee its accuracy and validity and cannot be held liable for any errors or omissions. Changes are periodically made to this book. You must consult your doctor or get professional medical advice before using any of the suggested remedies, techniques, or information in this book.

Upon using the information contained in this book, you agree to hold harmless the Author from and against any damages, costs, and expenses, including any legal fees potentially resulting from the application of any of the information provided by this guide. This disclaimer applies to any damages or injury caused by the use and application, whether directly or indirectly, of any advice or information presented, whether for breach of contract, tort, negligence, personal injury, criminal intent, or under any other cause of action.

You agree to accept all risks of using the information presented inside this book. You need to consult a professional medical practitioner in order to ensure you are both able and healthy enough to participate in this program.

Table of Contents

INTRODUCTION 1

CHAPTER 1: HOW TO STOP LYING TO YOURSELF AND EXPRESS YOUR FEELINGS TO OTHERS IN YOUR LIFE 5

CHAPTER 2: HABITS OF SELF-ACCEPTANCE THAT CAN IMPROVE WELL-BEING 18

CHAPTER 3: PSYCHOLOGY OF BULLIES PSYCHOLOGY OF BULLIES 29

CHAPTER 4: SELF-ESTEEM ESSENTIALS AND OTHER INFORMATION TO KNOW 46

CHAPTER 5: HOW TO LEARN TO RECOGNIZE DIFFICULT CONVERSATIONS AND HOW TO IDENTIFY THEM 53

CHAPTER 6: BOLDNESS: THE WAY TO GO 73

CHAPTER 7: THE REASONS WHY SELF-ESTEEM IS ESSENTIAL 84

CHAPTER 8: PRACTICING THE MOST EFFECTIVE METHOD TO PRACTICE 93

CHAPTER 9: BELIEVE YOU CAN 111

CHAPTER 10: WHAT IS THE REASON WOMEN HAVE A POOR SELF-IMAGE? 119

CHAPTER 11: LOOKING THE PART 132

CHAPTER 12: FINDING SELF-CONFIDENCE - WHAT IT WILL AFFECT YOU 137

CHAPTER 13: LIFE GOALS 153

CHAPTER 14: HEALTHY VS. LOW SELF-ESTEEM? 173

CONCLUSION 183

Introduction

Many people feel down at times in moment. It is important to recognize that feelings of low self-esteem could result from being treated badly by someone other than yourself. This could be in the past or the future it is a common feeling to take over whenever you feel threatened emotionally. A lack of self-esteem can be due to a person self-perception of him or her self. It is important to accept that this is a normal thing however, a flawed self-esteem is present for many people, especially those suffering from depression or phobias, delusional thoughts or psychosis or suffer from an health condition or disability. If you are in one of these situations it is likely that you'll feel bad about yourself a lot. Self-esteem issues will stop you from living the life you've always wanted to desires, and from doing what you've always wanted to do or even working towards your own goals.

It is your right to feel confident about yourself, however, it isn't an easy task to take on in particular when you're in the midst of stress due to problems to manage. When you're struggling with disabilities, have a difficult time exercising or when you are experiencing a situation where others treat you badly. When you are in these situations it's not difficult to fall into an downward spiral of low and low self-esteem. For instance you might start feeling a sense of shame whenever someone makes a snide comment about yourself, you're in a high-pressure situation from work or you find difficult to connect with your family members. In the next moment, you'll start to think about negative self-talk like," I'm no good". This will make you feel like you're not good enough and you could be doing something that could hurt someone else or yourself like getting high on alcohol , or even screaming at your children or your spouse. If you use and practice the suggestions and exercises included in the guide, you will be able to be sure to avoid doing the things that can make you feel even more miserable and perform the actions which will improve your confidence in yourself.

This book will give you suggestions for things could be done to make you feel completely confident about yourself and also to improve the level of self-esteem. When you put into practice the strategies that are in this book as well as other methods you develop following the reading of this book, you'll be able to see that you're not always able towards positive feelings about yourself. This is not unusual.

A gentle caution, please don't let these feelings stop you from feeling better about yourself. They will fade as you feel more confident about yourself. To help ease the stress, tell your loved ones like your family and friends, as well as your colleagues of the issues you're facing. Take a deep breath whenever you are able to. Engage in activities that give you the best relaxation for example, meditation or an enjoyable bath.

Chapter 1: How to Stop Lying to Yourself and Express Your Feelings To others in your life

Assertiveness is a skill in the social realm which requires training just like every other. It requires specific skills in communication, which allow us to effectively communicate our opinions limits, desires and desires to others. It is best to compare this ability as a muscle which needs to be worked in order to grow big and robust. The assertive people are those who can stand up for their beliefs without causing offence or sabotaging the opinions of other people. This requires us to strike the right direction, balancing between satisfying our own desires while respecting those of other people.

One of the most formidable adversaries, if not the most formidable enemy of assertiveness is self-deceit. Many times, we believe that we're happy with how things are in order to avoid causing a stir or causing a disturbance to people. It is common for us to live for long time in our lives in a state of denial about the things which cause us the most stress. Insufficient assertiveness is not only making us weaker as individuals. it completely affects our lives, causing us to be content and quietly accept the sometimes bleak reality we're confronted by.

To be more assertive in our beliefs and requirements, we should first establish what our demands and positions are. The assertive person is confident of what their position is on questions they confront and they know precisely what they want to get out of their lives. An inactive person can remain in a situation that causes suffering for a long time because the person does not have an notion of what he or she actually feels about the arrangement and what is required to feel content with the arrangement. A confident person is, however is able to pinpoint precisely what is causing the problem and know what would like to do instead.

In terms of cognitively, an assertive individual typically experiences less stressed than a passive person. They are not only more adept at dealing with thoughts of anxiety than others are and experience less anxiety overall probably due to the increased sense of control they have over their personal lives. The discipline and professionalism that assertive people exhibit to other people and situations can help them determine their golden middle between passive and aggressive. Through this path of behavior, the assertive person leads their life with greater confidence and self-esteem Never flinching to express their opinions or influence others to think in a way that is their own.

Conflict is the foundation of relationships. It is impossible to be involved in any way by other people without experiencing some type of conflict. If we find ourselves confronted by another person, there are two main choices: either we ignore our own viewpoint and just accept the view of the other. Or, we can respectfully and clearly express our opinion in a manner that we believe is appropriate to the end goal of solving the issue that caused the conflict. This is where a good amount of pragmatism will be required If we speak our minds that are not aimed at solving the problem in the first place, we will cause no harm and may even hurt the other party. Conflict should not be taken part in. That is that it should not be conducted solely for the sake of it as a hobby. When we are in conflict with people around us, we need to behave in a manner that lets us express our opinions, and may help to resolve the issue that is causing the dispute.

Being assertive is linked with a higher sense of autonomy, lower levels of depression and anxiety, as well as overall , better relationships. The social skills are often confused with aggression, however it is distinct from aggression because assertive individuals do not use their authority to intimidate or provoke others. They usually don't suffer from any behavior issues and generally do not lashing at other people. Being assertive, in contrast to being aggressive is more about protecting your own belongings from burning and less about igniting fires.

In the traditional sense, one must be able to satisfy two conditions for deceiving himself or herself 1. Self-deceivers must have different beliefs. They must purposely believe in a belief that is believed to be untrue. Sometimes we are having difficulties resolving things that arise in life that it is difficult to push ourselves to adhere to false beliefs, often because of a desire for security or control.

Rationalization is a psychological strategy is employed, whether conscious or not to justify or explain behavior or feelings that are polarizing with rational and rational reasoning. This can cause us to adhere to false beliefs under the basis that our beliefs are based on logic and rational thought patterns. We could defend the truthfulness of a close stance by using logic-based tricks, and rationalization can lead us to believe in our own assertions, regardless of how unlikely the beliefs we're fighting happen to be.

The rationale's foundation is typically discovered in socialization, fear personal biases, cognitive suppression. It is possible to rationalize either in a positive way or negatively which means that we have the option to view negative events positively and vice versa. Whatever the reasons behind rationalization or the direction that we rationalize this method is considered to be a coping strategy which is a thought pattern which is not in accordance with reality, and thus doesn't necessarily aid us.

Sometimes, our attachments to these false beliefs are rooted in emotion at the time of their beginning. When we are experiencing the most intense experiences that we are most vulnerable to deceitful self-talk. Anyone who is not experiencing any problems at this moment is less likely to being prone to self-deceiving thoughts because the person is not required to convince themselves of false beliefs to rationalize the reality. When reality is manageable our minds are able to accept reality as it is. When reality becomes too hard to handle that we begin to believe in self-deception.

We all make mistakes at times. Self-deceit is one of the easiest of an opportunity to get caught in However, what's difficult is to reverse its consequences after it is infiltrated into our mental patterns. Removing self-deception and the limiting beliefs is difficult due to the fact that once these patterns have been built into your mind, it is difficult to discern those thoughts that are triggered by these patterns from rational ones. In the process of separating our private truths from our fictional ones We are inevitably unable to see certain truths as lies or inflate falsehoods to be truths. Self-deceit leads to our whole integrated knowledge structures to be untrue and there is no line that can separate truth from lies.

It is possible to easily and succinctly review the more restrictive beliefs we have in order to determine where truth lies and where they are false. If thoughts we think of appear to be disconnected from reality (at at least in a way that appears to be) we must be aware of them and begin considering them in a critical manner and trying to come up with rational ideas to replace these thoughts and bring us closer to the truth. If we don't spend the time to examine these thought patterns, which are often faulty They will eventually dominate our lives, dragging us to ignore the truth that is always before our eyes.

The emotions of our lives and the associated with them are the most important thing to us psychologically. They makes us who we are and are the only thing that guide us in life and are what make it worthwhile to live. If we aren't transparent about our emotions and are unable to convey them to ourselves or other people, then we're not living honest lives. The honesty that we exhibit is, however easier to talk about than actually achieved.

To be more transparent with ourselves and others we must first acknowledge that we're not in the wrong to feel the emotions that we do, regardless of what they may be. Although our feelings may sometimes be in contrast to the situation at hand however, they are a fundamental part of us and deserve our focus. If someone is angry about the traffic that he is experiencing, the idea of throwing their cup of coffee outside is not a good idea however the instinct to do this is triggered by his anger for a short period of time is not to be dismissed. We're not always the best judge of how we react to situations however, we're usually acting as the legislators of our own emotions, therefore it is always a good idea to understand what emotions try to tell us.

Genuineness and honesty are two of the most important traits for the person. Whatever the extent to which people are offended by our honesty It is this honesty can allow us to be as a real person at all times, therefore it shouldn't be ignored or discarded. Being pleasant and agreeable are both very attractive traits however they aren't always required and aren't always the most appropriate methods to conduct yourself. Sometimes, allowing ourselves to be honest and sincere as we can, will demonstrate that we're more irritable and difficult to surround ourselves with than we believed, but there's no problem with being disagreeable when they are required and to feel at ease within our own skin, we must embrace the darker aspects of our personality. This frees us from the shackles of respect and helps us improve our psychological well-being However, failing to do it will result in an inability to accept ourselves and a reluctance to show those more "honest" aspects of ourselves.

Authenticity is the extent that a person's actions align with their values or preferences regardless of external circumstances. Anyone whose actions differ in the sense of their purpose from the beliefs of his or her own or values is considered to be unauthentic. On the other hand, one who is acting in accordance with his or her own principles is believed to be authentic. The quality of authenticity that is evident in actions is distinct from the notion of external influences because the quality of our actions can only be judged by the similarity of our values and beliefs. The notion of authenticity can be described in the old saying "know your self," but should rather be expanded to "be yourself."

If we base our decisions on the goals and purposes of external influences we rob ourselves of our personal agency that is typically restricted in and of its own. Inauthenticity in the sense that we are acting solely for the requirements of others is unproductive and in two ways It does not meet our own needs however, it doesn't satisfy the people we're trying to improve as they are not satisfied with the amount of assistance they receive from a third party.

Many postmodernist thinkers believe that we are simply cultural objects, whose ideas and actions are influenced by the general decisions of the people in our lives. Although the degree to which this notion is true is debateable, what is certain is the fact that we're constantly influenced by the people in our lives, for better or worse. This is the reason we need to think about our own desires first, as the desires of others can take over our thoughts as well as our personal motives if we're not mindful of the things we spend our time doing.

Chapter 2: Habits of Self-Acceptance that Can Improve Well-being

Self-acceptance is the process of knowing your weaknesses and strengths, forming an opinion about your strengths, value abilities, skills and feeling content with who you are in the present, despite the flaws, shortcomings and past mistakes. You can also attempt to improve yourself. If you are able to accept yourself for who the person you truly are, then you develop self-love and self-understanding. Because of that your mental well-being and self-esteem improves.

The most effective way to cultivate self-acceptance and improve your self-esteem, well-being and self-development (and consequently peace and success) is to cultivate self-love.

These habits and practices can assist you in achieving this goal:

11: Get daily self-care

The majority of our time working to meet the demands of our employers, partners and spouses, children and community. This is why a lot people don't make the effort to allocate time for ourselves. This is normal because when life gets busy and you're constantly working, taking time to pursue things you enjoy seems to be a waste of time. It's not!

Based on Kristen Martinez, a licensed psychotherapist, committing a small portion of your day to yourself and making use of this time to do things you enjoy, can lead to a greater feeling of well-being and an exercise in self-love.

The way Jim Kwik noted, "we get tired not because we've accomplished excessively, but because we've not done enough of what ignites a fire within our own." To ignite an inner light state, you should practice self-care every day by committing a significant portion of your daytime time doing something you truly love or are interested in. The more you practice this more often, the better you feel about yourself and the more your self-esteem will rise.

12 Do not compare yourself with others.

If you adopt this practice and stick to it, you will experience immediate improvements in your self-esteem (self-worth as well as self-worth).

We spend a significant portion time comparing our personality life, achievements, and lives to the lives of our close and friends from the social world.

If you are comparing yourself with someone else, particularly when you compare your accomplishments with that of a family member or acquaintance, you are in essence disproving your individuality, claiming you are uniquely you and thus have distinct goals and talents, weaknesses or strengths. Due to this "comparison disease that we all suffer from, many of us have a tendency to spend the majority of the day believing that we're "less than" and competing in a race that we can't be successful because nobody else can be'you' more than you."

When you next find yourself comparing your accomplishments against those of a friend on the internet, remember your self that the sole person who you ought to be competing with is the person who you were yesterday.

13: Be mindful of your self-talk

A low self-esteem can be a result of beating and berating yourself. This is itself a result of self-deflection.

If you find that the majority all of your thinking is negative, the habit of living that was that were discussed previously will aid in this realization--make an effort to change these thoughts into positive more compassionate, loving ones.

If, for instance, you think often "no regardless of what I try or how hard I try at it, I am unable to be successful in relationships with females," doubt the validity of that thought by searching for evidence that supports or refutes it. You can then replace your negative thoughts with a positive, caring thought like "the more I test different strategies and strategies, the closer I am to achieving my personal goals in dating, women, or relationships."

If you do this regularly, or whenever you can that becomes less difficult by focusing on it with conscious intention--your inner voice transforms into an optimistic one that promotes feelings of well-being, self-confidence, peace as well as personal accomplishment as well as satisfaction over the way which you're directing your life.

14: Get enough rest

Sleep is an essential human requirement, and is one of the most neglected self-love practices. Due to our busy lifestyles our lives, we don't have enough sleep which is an injustice because sleep deficiency can cause a host of health issues like chronic anxiety and stress (and depression) and heart disease, diabetes and many more, including an unending feeling of fatigue (being depleted of energy) and lack of motivation in your day-to-day activities.

Achieving 7-10 hours of rest every single day isn't an act of self-interest. It's a self-love act that improves your health and feelings of peace and since being well-rested increases your energy levels, getting enough rest also results in increased productivity and energy that means a better ability to make decisions that improve your odds of success and, as you've probably guessed the feeling of getting something boosts your self-esteem.

15: Journal daily

Writing is among the most cathartic practices that is available.

If you make journaling a regular part of your daily routine by writing down each day, night and at every opportunity you have, you will experience unpleasant or negative thoughts onto paper and off of your mind. Having allowed them to grow which could have resulted in negative effects on your psyche/spiritual state.

The reflection that comes from journaling every day can help you be better aware of own needs as well as weaknesses, strengths goals, benefits as well as the disadvantages. This enhances your perception of selfand, in the words of Alison Ledgerwood, a professor at the University of California, it increases your feelings of gratitude, as well as your physical health.

16 Relaxation: Try to practice awareness

Relaxed awareness is like mindfulness and conscious intention. The major distinction between the two is that in a state of an open mind, the goal is to cultivate present awareness and acceptance of what is happening right now.

The practice, for instance, requires you to be aware of your own judgments and self-criticism, your thoughts, feelings or weaknesses. and accept them without judgment without having to judge yourself or embark on any type of changes.

Relaxed awareness is basically the ability to be aware of the world as it is , without the desire to alter what is happening at the time. If you practice it consistently it allows you to be conscious of your body, thoughts, mind, and emotions, as well as their constantly changing nature.

For a chance to practice try it, just shut your eyes. Rather instead of focusing on your breath be conscious of everything happening in the moment including your thoughts, feelings and sensations, for example. Watch your mind and you can be sure that your personal well-being will improve.

17: Let go of "should-should." "should" mentality

The majority of us live the majority of our lives tied to the notion of: "I should be this or that, I must perform this or that I should have accomplished this or that, by the time I am reading this, I must be feeling X or Y" and so on.

By committing yourself to this attitude, you will only contribute to the competition game which is, as we said is harmful to your self-esteem, confidence in yourself confidence, peace of mind confidence in yourself, and your chances of achievement.

To grab yourself by the bootstraps, begin the journey of self-growth and break free from the "should" attitude, engage in daily mindfulness and mindful intention. These exercises help make you aware of situations where you may use phrases like "I must be _____."

From this state of awareness and awareness, you are able to connect with your goal and what you're doing and the reason you're doing it. If your intentions do not match your goals or goals, or what you are trying to achieve, you can change your mindset to transform the inner dialogue that is causing you to feel negative into positive inner conversation that can lead to personal development and a higher confidence in yourself and peace. It also increases the likelihood of the achievement of your personal goals.

18: Try daily realism

The type of realism that we're talking about is being realistic about your abilities, but particularly about what you are able to and can't accomplish within a certain time frame.

Self-esteem issues often arise out of feeling unworthy and unworthy, which is the result of eating the more you're able to chew, or being too demanding of your friends and family members, as well as being disappointed and depressed when things don't work out the way you planned.

Goals are an awesome method of living a life that is purposeful however, when it is your intention to reach specific goals or objectives be sure to ask yourself "Am I realistic about what I can achieve in this time frame?" If not, change your priorities and schedule to allow you more time to accomplish things that will fill your life with joy and positivity which are the things which lead to self-esteem confidence in yourself, and personal achievement.

Chapter 3: Psychology Of Bullies

Psychology Of Bullies

The ability to confront bullies, especially as we grow older will help us recover from any emotional trauma. A particularly difficult aspect when dealing with bullies in adulthood the bully tactics are often less obvious than children who bully.

The majority of the information found in this book, and the information that is available, is focused on teaching us how to effectively deal with bullies. But this chapter will adopt a different perspective and will focus on the psychological reasons behind the bullying behavior. Examining bullying in this way can help you break free from such assaults as you'll gain an awareness of their flaws. Although all forms of bullying are harmful and cause us to feel guilty We should take them as an opportunity to learn from the experience through which we are in a position to improve ourselves.

The common perception of bullies generally is that they are unhappy with themselves and feel extremely insecure and thus find an outlet for their emotions by causing others to feel pain and causing them to feel discomfort. They are usually characterized by feelings like helplessness and fear.

But, more studies into the subject have revealed that this might not be the only motivating factor behind bullying and that they're also unaware of their own hurts. If you've been in the presence of people who bullied you in the past then, you'll not recall they were weak or unsecure. In fact, they were seen as domineering or powerful.

The most recent information in this field indicates that bullies target other people as a way to conceal their most intense feelings from them. When they attack others they forget what they are feeling. They devise strategies to cause their victims to feel negative emotions, such as humiliation, shame, and inadequacy and other emotions that they hide from themselves. Since they're unconsciously associated by these emotions, this is why they have a tendency to instill these feelings in other people. They are adept at not consciously identifying the weaknesses of their victims and fears in order to take advantage of their weaknesses and vulnerabilities. These attacks bring out negative emotions of the victims, which they're not scared of and are unable to confront themselves.

In focusing on other people and putting them down, it provides the bully with an emotional rush by causing feelings of power, control and excitement. If they are putting others down and trying to avoid their own emotions they forget about getting themselves up and instead, replay these emotions by the abuse of their victims. They don't usually feel guilty for their actions toward their victims since they feel happy. But these aren't real positive feelings.

Because all emotions are energy that cannot be destroyed. The negative emotions of bullies require an outlet , and the only way to be let go is by engaging in them or using others to exploit them. The bully can't make themselves vulnerable enough to bear their own hurt and emotions Therefore, they provide the bully a way to express their feelings by the bullying of other people.

The reason why bullies are weak. They are unable to confront themselves and their own suffering. Many suffer from deeply-felt shame that they've never been able to speak about.

Repressing Feelings

We all adjust ourselves so that we do not have to feel negative emotions like shame. It is one of the most damaging emotions we feel, and that's why we develop ways of being able to avoid facing the issue. The most frequently employed methods of repression can be classified as follows:

- Isolation. Certain people just avoid people and social settings so that they don't have to feel their own hurt feelings. We are most vulnerable around others and by avoiding them, we feel secure because our repression defenses will not be attacked. This allows us to live life without ever having to confront those parts of us that are the most frightening to us. The fear of our deepest feelings being revealed causes us to avoid social interaction, that leads to an atmosphere of isolation. We conceal our feelings from the world by cloaking ourselves.

- The avoidance response. Like being isolated, some individuals will trigger an avoidance reaction where they engage in an addictive habit to keep from having to face themselves. This could include eating and alcohol, drug use or sex, exercise, or any other distractions.

Self-blame is another way of avoiding. It can also lead to self-harm , either mentally or physically. Self-blaming behavior has negative implications for self-esteem and self respect.

The act of bullying is one of the most damaging reactions to shame. A person is psychologically frightened (unconsciously) due to their fears, and thus attacks other to replace these feelings with ones of power and authority.

We all know that bad emotions aren't pleasant to feel. When we feel frequently when we are young and we are unable to bear the pain they cause, which is why unproductive ways of dealing with these emotions are created. It's just an way to get rid of these emotions. It is not connected with the person being bullied. The bully is able to spot a flaw in the character of their victim. A victim of bullying might also be denial of their own hurt feelings and this makes them a victim. The bully is unaware of these emotions.

In this way We can recognize that any act of violence against us is a sign that we are not perfect and must work on, however, the person who is abused also has issues. The victim is afraid of what lurks within their own subconscious and lacks the courage to confront it. In their core, they are scared. When we encounter bullies, they can appear confident and could even be popular with other people. The confidence they display is typically an illusion. We all have an external persona however for bullies, it can help protect them by creating an image of them as confident and confident. However, this isn't a strong confidence that's often developed to protect.

How to Guard Against Bullies

Knowing the psychological reasons that drives bullying can help us deal with bullies when confronted by them. It is crucial not to get caught up in feeling empathy for them. This could hinder your ability to handle your situation in a manner that is safe for yourself. Instead, by understanding their motivations this can aid in creating an apprehension of the person who is bullying you and their behavior. If this occurs it is likely that the bully will be able to pick up on it through our non-verbal behaviors and, consequently, be unable to exploit us. If they start to view us as a person in a different way, they might be unable to spot the same weaknesses in us.

The bullies have to learn how to confront their own demons and realize that making other people victimized isn't acceptable. When we stand up to bullies, they may be forced to confront themselves, which means we're actually helping them as well as ourselves an favor. They need guidance in navigating their feelings of guilt, shame and anger. If everybody stood up to them, they'd eventually have to be able to recognize how to deal with themselves. However, at the same time it is important to acknowledge that we are wounded, which makes us easy victims. We must take a step back to address our own personal pain that will allow us to improve all the relationships we have with others.

By understanding and learning about the psychological nature of bullies It can help the victim to stop their attack. We begin to recognize their weaknesses than they do, and this is something that bullies be able to sense. When they understand their motives and motives, they will lose power over us.

Self-Sabotage

Our common sense will tell us that we choose to do what makes us content. But we tend to do the opposite and in a way, subconsciously try to undermine ourselves in the most critical aspects of life. One of the most frequent self-defeating behaviors is that we are prone to blame external factors for our troubles. This could be with your partner, a employee, boss or even a family member, when in reality, the fault could be on us.

The non-assertive behavior is basically an act of self-sabotage. We act in a manner that hinders us from obtaining the things we require. We really need love and validation, but those things must originate from ourselves. Since these beliefs are triggered without conscious thought, we are not realize why we do the things we do. These negative thought patterns, like not being sufficient, acquired from childhood, are the programming that we use throughout life as we grow older. We aren't trying to transfer the blame to the people who created them since as mature adults , we must assume full responsibility for ourselves.

If we can begin to identify these self-defeating behaviors, we can begin to recognize that we blame anyone else in any part of our lives. Another thing we could concentrate on is which parts of our life that we are putting off? Who do we hide our feelings from? We tend to avoid confronting the issues that must be resolved by using various ways like alcohol or food, TV and time-wasting shopping and more. These things can distract us from confronting ourselves and our problems directly. These behavior patterns should be easily discernible if we're being honest and sincere with ourselves.

As we get older and begin to become more conscious,, we can often detect that something isn't quite right. Usually, it is through feelings of sadness or anger. To track these feelings things, I would suggest keeping a diary and recording your day-to-day events. This allows us to start to recognize certain themes and then detach from them and processing them simultaneously.

After a few minutes of recording these thoughts, you'll begin to notice patterns you made as a child , but that persist to influence your daily life. It's almost like a prison, which was constructed from the earliest programming's. As we mature, which assists in keeping them in place. It makes us feel restricted within the boundaries of them. To break free from these patterns, you need to begin to observe them in your personal characteristics. You can learn to do this by meditation. While we are meditating thoughts come and go Try to look at and studying every thought, while observing and being aware of the inner dynamics.

You might start to notice patterns of rejection, patterns of abandonment or a pattern that permits others to walk over you. Once you've acknowledged this you will begin to realize that you don't need to participate in any behaviour that causes people to behave badly towards you. When you recognize patterns that repeat and the effects they cause and how they affect you, you can learn that you aren't required to be a part of a behavior that causes you to feel uneasy or consequences. There is a certain amount of control over our behavior. We can express a message whenever we see patterns, for example "this is an old pattern that I do not need anymore, so I let it go, I forgive it, I let it go and allow it to go. everything is good, it's good. Everyone is doing their best as they can. This pattern isn't mine and no longer belongs to me'. When we notice an issue, we are able to self-correct it.

Every act we do helps improve our awareness of ourselves as well as any other similar patterns that we may have. Through writing about them and delving into where they originated We can then begin to change them into new perspectives. The only way to progress is to overcome resistance. Avoiding feelings, or to ignore themwill only cause them to be repressed and make them worse.

Another illustration of this can be that of romantic relationship and romantic relationships. It's common for people to be able to be themselves and comfortable with people they aren't attracted to. When confronted with an intense attraction to the person they are considering for a relationship the person might find it difficult to communicate in the same manner. The attraction could derail the possibility of something better. The sabotaging process is usually resulted from feelings of inferiority and self-esteem issues. If we don't believe we're worthy of others' love and attention, then we'll behave in a manner that makes us unworthy of being able to receive the same.

In other instances it is possible to be in a relationship with a perfect partner, but we undermine it by arguments or other methods which pushes the other away. This could occur in our professional lives as well and we might be offered a fantastic chance, but somehow we fail to make it work. Like we said earlier, we believe that we all would like to be happy and have a prosperous life, but if this is something we've never experienced or planned for, the thought of achieving it may become overwhelming. Perhaps we've grown up in situations where we had to put on with the negative experiences and aren't in a position or prepared to experience genuine happiness, if it does not feel right to us. If you reflect on your life and find that you haven't had numerous experiences in which you were completely content and content, the chances of having this experience in your current life is likely to be minimal at the very least. Humans tend to stick with the things it is familiar with as survival is the main mental programming that the brain has to perform. Each new act is perceived as a threat that is not known to us. Due to our unconscious programming, we tend to pick what we are used to, even if it's unfavorable, in contrast to what's good and satisfying since it's brand unfamiliar and unsettling to us. This isn't what we been expecting before. So, what we'd like to achieve is often extremely challenging and difficult. Not only do we must contend with the external challenges, but also the inner difficulties of experiencing something completely thrilling and new.

The unconscious needs to be prepared for the new behavior It is possible to do this through visualisation. Similar to a computer our minds are only running pre-programmed programs, unless of course, it is upgraded. Thus, adopting the new habit or even pursuing the things we desire can be uncertain and even frightening. We must be open to new things, which brings with the fear of losing in the event that we fail to achieve the goals we have set for ourselves. Self-defeating behavior can leave us feeling unhappy but secure, since at least we know what we can expect and , more importantly, have confidence in our abilities.

Be conscious of the self-defeating behaviors you are committing when you next interact with anyone. This will allow you to be aware of your own actions. When we begin paying the actions we're taking or if we're acting in ways that could be destined create problems, we will be able to recognize our own behavior and then, through practice, learn to behave differently. This type of behavior is usually observed when we're with people who whom we want to impress. If we consider and anticipate another person's behaviour (what we're used to) This can increase the resistance to acting differently, as we are afraid that others will notice that we're being different.

Chapter 4: Self-Esteem Essentials and Other information to know

If you look at yourself in the mirror and you think or positive thoughts about yourself or you would like to go away and disappear, that's self-esteem. If you are in a crowd and confidently look at other people around you or pray that no one even notices that you are there it is self-esteem.

Naturally, the notion of self-esteem is more than the basics. But, it provides an overview of how it affects your everyday self-image and the way you interact with other people.

Self-esteem has been accepted by many for more than 100 years. It was first introduced in the late William James, who is known as the psychologist's father. Self-esteem is a part of self-concept that includes many different components.

The History of Self-Esteem as an Idea

William James was an American philosopher and psychologist who lived from 1842 until 1910. James was the man who introduced many of the key concepts that psychology believes and is a constant reminder of even today. One of these concepts that is now referred to as self-esteem defined as self and the different parts within the self. They include the components of the self. These comprise the material, social and spiritual self, as well as"the "Pure Self" (1). These four elements, along their emotions, emotions they generate and the behaviors that occur, constitute the self. The social self is that is closely linked to self-esteem because it focuses on how the person interacts with the world at large as well as how we perceive and internalize the social reactions to our appearance and actions.

Based on this introduction written by James the psychologists started to create more elaborate theories and models of self-esteem and its significance to our thinking and behavior.

The Rosenberg self-esteem Scale (RSES)

"Dr. Morris Rosenberg was interested in self-image, especially for adolescents. Rosenberg wrote his book about the image of self that adolescents have. Rosenberg developed a test that can be used to study an individual's self-esteem by analyzing the answers they provide. The test uses an overall scale of 30 with different points assigned to each answer in the tests (2). There are four options in response to each statement that include strongly agree, accept, disagree and disagree. The questions focus on your feelings about yourself as well as how you perceive yourself in comparison to others, and your opinions about your worth in the world, and the amount of positive attributes you possess.

The statements include:

I believe that I am an individual of value and am at the least at a level with other people.

I think I'm blessed with several excellent attributes.

Overall I tend to believe that I'm not good enough.

I can do things just as many other people.

I am not sure I have anything to be proud of.

I have a positive outlook towards myself.

Overall. I am content with my self-esteem.

I would like to be more respectful of myself.

I definitely feel unimportant often.

Sometimes, I feel I'm not very great at all.

The test is just 10 questions in length, all of which will have different points for the answers, based on the nature of the test. Questions that are more negative have the highest score in the case of "strongly oppose," while the highest value for other questions is "strongly concur" (3).

The RSES can be used to determine whether your self-esteem falls within an "normal" interval (15 to 25) or "low" at 15 or less (4).

Information About Self-Esteem

There are some facts regarding self-esteem which are essential to know to understand what to do when you're struggling with low self-esteem and want to boost your self-esteem to increase.

The first thing to note is that there is different kinds of self-esteem. Every person has a global self-esteem. This is the way you perceive your self in general. You also have particular self-esteem for every role you take in the world and for each obligation that you have in your life (parenting and your work and as your partner)(5). In addition, each kind of self-esteem specific to you has its own level of significance in the life of. The effect it has on your global self-esteem is contingent on the importance that this particular aspect of self-esteem is for you.

Another interesting aspect about self-esteem - and one that is crucial to the efforts we are making here is that self-esteem can fluctuate from day to day and even between hours hour(5). So, it is possible to create new habits that will help boost your self-esteem. You can incorporate those practices during specific times of the your day, if you observe that these times lower your self-esteem significantly for no reason.

Self-esteem isn't related to the physical attractiveness of a person. You can be the most attractive looker in the world but still be lacking self-esteem if you view things negative thoughts and don't make an effort to look at events and situations positively.

In the end, it's crucial to realize that those who are self-confident do not necessarily have a superior situation than those who have low self-esteem. Narcissists have a very high perception of self-worth, however they are also more likely to be hurt and influenced with insults, or comments that weren't meant to be insults, but were interpreted as such (5).

Chapter 5: How to Learn to recognize difficult conversations and how to Identify Them

Four words are in the English language that people have come to fear when hearing in conjunction, especially from a boss or romantic partner, or any other close relationship: We need to speak. It is not a pleasant thing to hear the word targeted at them, since it's always followed by a difficult discussion that is:

The emotions are often charged, provoking or causing frustration.

It is awash with details that no one would like to hear about negative information or critique.

An issue that can inspire shifts that people aren't aware of or aren't prepared for.

It is inevitable to have difficult conversations in life, whether at work, with close family members and at the home of your family. A lot of people around the world struggle to lead or start in a challenging conversation and it's not common to meet someone who does not like being part of these conversations (especially those who find themselves in situations where they're an integral part of the daily routine like counseling or management).

While you might not be able to avoid challenging discussions, there are many methods to help make these less painful, stressful and emotionally draining for all those involved. We'll be discussing this in greater detail during the entire book. However, prior to discussing the specifics of different situations that require discussion it is essential to know the nature of difficult conversations, the reasons they occur and how you can ensure that you're ready before you get into one.

What is a difficult conversation?

The details of this question will differ for each individual However, the most commonly accepted definition of a difficult discussion is as one in which the subjects to be addressed or the goals to be accomplished or issues that are to be resolved could trigger an emotional reaction from the people involved, and causing the feeling of stress for the person who is expected to initiate or steer the discussion.

How to Know When A Need for a difficult conversation is Necessary

There are many issues that are solvable or addressed, as well as questions that can be answered , and concerns which are addressed with out the need to create a fuss, and simply by delivering a mail by email or text. These are situations where an employee has violated the rules of an assignment and has to change their actions or a small change is required which doesn't cause any annoyance or cause stress. This isn't the type of management for situations that should be employed to:

More complex issues that require many individuals or involve a range of possible implications.

Complex issues that have the potential of creating confusion or require clarification.

Important issues that can affect the personal conduct of individuals or emotional responses in a stressful situation or environment.

Every situation that requires an immediate and specific touch to bring about the desired outcome and avoid exacerbating current situation.

Professional Tip: Create A Set of Rules based on proven techniques

Over time, you will realize that most of your guidelines and rules for handling difficult conversations stem from your own experience, however making a simple "Difficult conversations Management List" to have in your pocket is among the most frequently cited and widely used tips when it comes to understanding how to handle conflict or uncomfortable situations regardless of the location or subject you're discussing.

The process of planning an intervention is among the most frequent instances of when an individual (or group) has determined that the best way to convey their worries to the person they are concerned about is to invite other people who have a close relationship with them join in a peaceful discussion in a safe environment. The guidelines for handling interventions are the same for handling any challenging situation. This is something that we will discuss more in the next chapter, as one of the fundamentals of dealing with difficult conversations everywhere however some of the top things to start your personalized "Difficult Conversations Management List" using include:

Proven and researched methods for many difficult conversations and determining which ones are most effective in creating a secure and safe space.

Always be friendly regardless of whether it's an interaction that involves negative feedback or the discussion of inappropriate conduct.

Making sure that everyone is actively participating and heard, while ensuring making sure that everyone is listening and engaging.

Establishing a framework for the discussion (what subjects are discussed in order of when, and determining how long each person can speak uninterrupted so everyone gets the chance to hear) and an outline of the goals you'd like to achieve.

Although having a simple set of guidelines to aid in planning and organizing difficult conversations prior to beginning the process to ease it is beneficial but it won't always offer the right answers or strategies you require to handle every scenario. If you encounter situations similar to these, it's crucial to have the experience and the patience to make changes when needed.

Different kinds of difficult conversations

The conversation can be difficult and is a natural aspect of human interactions that is usually inevitable, with each one of them presenting its own particular challenges and stress to the people who participate. Some of the most popular kinds of difficult conversations are:

Dispensing Bad News: This is one of the most challenging conversations you can be having in a private or professional context. In this kind of discussion there is data that needs to be disclosed to a person, or a group of people that you're sure will make them feel upset. This could be in a smaller capacity , such as displeasure at not being able to meet a specific objective or in a more extensive situation, such as needing to inform someone of losing a loved one.

Cut Off the Band-Aid: This is among of the most suggested methods of delivering bad news. This doesn't mean that you should be blunt and unkind (particularly when you are aware are emotionally charged) however, rather be proactive and clear in how you talk when speaking up.

Do not fudge the issue or avoid engaging in the conversation. When it comes time to share bad information, timing is essential. It is best to be calm and manage your stress in the event that you are the one to deliver the message. When you are able to have your own feelings in your hands, the quicker you will be able plan and conduct the conversation, and end it for yourself as well as others involved.

The other person may be incorrect: This kind of difficult conversation is of the most depressing situations people can have. If someone is wrong in their actions or with the information they've got but is unable to hear or communicate with any other person on the subject It creates a problem which has a low chance of getting resolved in a timely manner without careful forward movement.

Also known as an oppositional discussion pattern, this kind of behavior can get out of control if it is not closely watched throughout the discussion. In this response pattern that you're trying to convince with accurate information is unwilling to admit the error or misunderstanding, no matter the evidence or information that has been presented.

The more serious cases go one step further and do not just refuse to admit that they're wrong but attempt to put their untrue opinions onto the person leading the discussion.

Another crucial point to keep in mind in this type of conversation is that there's a the difference between talking about and disagreeing.

There is no guarantee that everyone will have the same opinion on every topic or concept discussed in the course of a conversation. It is essential for you to open yourself to differing views (particularly in the case of seeking solutions to complicated problems).

One way to discern the difference between fighting and when someone is simply expressing an opinion is to recognize that the latter is likely to bring about some form of progress, whereas the former can lead to the conversation in circles , with the other person simply repeating their opinion without listening to what's being said.

Be judicious with your words The best method to deal with this type of challenging conversation is to ensure that no matter how someone else responds or speaks to the words being spoken it is maintained a calm tone, professional manner and a straight manner of speaking. The right language to use is about understanding the subject matter that must be addressed, the context and tone that is appropriate for the kind that you are having a conversation in, as well as recognizing that regardless of how carefully and thoroughly you handle the situation, you'll never be able to predict completely or control the way in which another person will respond.

Requesting a Change of behavior or status A conversation like this is among the most frequently encountered in every industry and. The most frequent examples include parents talking to children at any stage about negative behaviour such as skipping school, or supervisors talking to employees about workplace misconduct.

Listen and Be Helpful Be a Supportive Listener manage this kind of discussion is by being as transparent as you can about your issues (without engaging emotionally) and offer possible solutions rather than merely making a fuss, and ensure the person with whom you're talking is aware that they are able to ask questions during the discussion, but that you'll also be available to support their progress or concerns after the conversation has ended.

Questions to Ask Before You Get involved in a difficult conversation

If you're the person who initiated it, or in the position of leading it, or you are a participant there are some important questions you need to be able to answer before you get involved in a challenging conversation.

What do I hope to achieve with the dialogue that I have established during this conversation?

This is a crucial question for those who have to handle difficult conversations to understand prior to starting , as it's the best method to keep track of the progress made and remain focused in the event that emotions begin to rise high and the participants get off-topic.

This is crucial for those participating in difficult conversations and need to consider asking themselves questions as it helps you determine what to say and also what questions you should ask during the conversation.

This might not be an option if the discussion was not announced in advance or if the subject was not mentioned on the invitation (whether it was verbal or written).

Don't be afraid to inquire about the topic and purpose of the discussion once you realize it and take some time to collect your thoughts prior to your scheduled time.

How secure and comfortable do you feel to the venue, timing and the other participants in the discussion?

If you feel uncomfortable regarding the location, time or the way in which your discussion has been conducted It is crucial to voice your concerns. The main purpose of any uncomfortable conversation is to promote open communication.

There's a good chance that if you're not comfortable, people around you are too. If people feel uncomfortable in their own skin, they're less likely to speak their opinions in a candid and honest manner. Based on previous experiences How do you believe you'll be able control your emotions in this discussion?

Are there any steps you can do prior to the discussion to ensure a better mental state for you?

If there is an issue that is sensitive to discuss do you think it is possible to approach the discussion by keeping an open mind? refrain from arguing with others when they aren't in agreement or have negative remarks?

Are you in the correct mental and emotional condition to be able to take part in this discussion?

Be in a good mindset before beginning the conversation as it will affect several aspects such as how productive the conversation will be, how you react when people become emotional and how present you'll be throughout the discussion.

Professional Tip: Do Not be Reluctant to Delegate, However, Be aware of when it's necessary.

Discords that are difficult to handle can be emotionally charged regardless of how much the leaders try to keep everyone cool and focused. Whatever time you've had to prepare and how well prepared prior to the event, or how familiar you are in different kinds of challenging conversations, there are discussions or situations that you're not the best equipped to manage. In these situations it is essential to select the appropriate person to do the job and assist them in preparing for being the one who leads the conversation .

Although delegation is an important technique to master (particularly in business or professional environments) it is essential to keep in mind that there's the difference between delegating task and not doing it. If you're not able to deal with conflict well or becomes emotionally easily, it might be tempting to let an individual in the helm. But, this is an unwise response to stressful situations that could result in more severe issues with communication when used in a routine manner.

Here are some questions you can consider before delegating a difficult conversation to another person:

What is the reason I am delegating this conversation?

In the case of some people, the reason might be that they don't have the appropriate knowledge or understanding of the subject or purpose of the discussion. Some may have to delegate due to their relationship or past with the other the people in the conversation.

The inability to control the emotions of one's self and fear of confrontation aren't reasons to give someone else the reins of a conflict. When these (or similar motives) are the reasons you think of when you ask the question, rather than delegating the responsibility it is better for you and those who are involved to figure out ways to work without a fight and to talk in a non-judgmental manner.

Who do I delegate the task to competent to lead it to achieve the desired result?

Before transferring the control of an issue to another person, it's essential to understand their abilities and skills, as well as how they can be utilized to achieve goals effectively and address issues that have to be addressed within the context of the circumstance.

What should I do to sure that the individual I'm delegating the task responsibility to is prepared?

If you're not able to conduct the conversation by yourself the best way to handle it is (and the only way) to ensure that the person who is taking your place is as prepared as they can be to handle any issue that might be raised or questions which may arise.

One of the most effective method to achieve this is that you have a face-to-face meeting concerning the conversation and the outcome you're looking for, and any other predictable elements that could impact how successful the meeting will go. While it might be more convenient to email or converse over via phone, a face-to face meeting gives both parties a sense of certainty regarding the way the conversation is scheduled to unfold as well as allowing each party to ask questions in the event that there's something unclear or not understood from previous conversations, and also provides many other advantages which can only be obtained by having a face-to-face meeting.

It is not always the case that difficult conversations will be preceded by a period that is long enough to allow this. In these instances the best method to proceed is to ensure that you can be reached by the person who is in charge at any point during the discussion for any inquiries or to express concerns. This may include responding to texts or emails that are made during the discussion or contacting the leader delegated to you during scheduled breaks during the course of the session.

If you now have an understanding of the kinds of situations need difficult conversations and how you can identify and handle these, we'll talk in-depth about the basics of Difficult Conversations , and how you can not view them as everyday stressors, but instead effective communication tools that help all those that are

Chapter 6: Boldness: The Way to Go

"Freedom lies in being bold."

Robert Frost

If you've lived an average life, it's time to step up and be assertive. This book is designed for those who's biggest challenge is finding the courage to stand up for themselves, regardless of the circumstances that require it.

Be confident and courageous. There's a possibility that you're quaking in your own psyche but the world doesn't need to be aware. Take control of your shyness and become the confident person you're supposed to be. Take a examine yourself before attending a party and remind yourself that you're a strong as well-behaved person. While you're there Introduce yourself to someone that you've never seen before. Take a look and keep your head straight. Talk to him about his experiences. You'll breathe an exhale of satisfaction when you realize you survived the incident without any serious consequence.

Do things that scare you. The more you are able to practice doing things you're afraid about, the less frightening they'll be. If you're scared of making calls to someone you don't have a great relationship with Practice it until you feel comfortable. Courage isn't to avoid fear but to be able to experience fear and then take action regardless.

If you're assertive, you will get what you would like. When you assert yourself you increase confidence in yourself and boost self-esteem. You are aware of and can understand your emotions. You also gain the respect of your peers. It is a natural win-win scenario if you're bold. Being assertive and bold can help you build genuine and respecting relationships.

Here are some steps on how to assert yourself and be bold:

Utilize "I" assertions.

If you are using I-statements, you'll seem less and less accusatory. Instead of saying "You are certainly incorrect" You can instead use phrases like "I do not agree".

Be honest about your needs and thoughts.

If you are looking to increase confidence in yourself and earn the respect of others, you need to know how to convey your emotions and what you want. Don't assume that others are aware of what your needs and desires are. If you want to communicate your thoughts, make sure to express them in an a respectful and honest manner.

Learn to be able to say no.

If you're uncomfortable in the proposal, you can say no. It is important to realize it is acceptable. Do not be concerned about being selfish. In this instance it is important to prioritise your needs.

Certain people I've worked with have found it very difficult to say no. It's simply not their style to be a person who refuses to accept someone's request. They're extremely gratified. They'd rather experience any inconvenience and stress themselves out than let someone down. Should this be a major issue to you, I'll provide you with some phrases you can apply to make you be more comfortable with saying"no. This exercise might seem odd initially however, I guarantee that it will be helpful by practicing it for a long time. Find yourself face-to-face with an mirror to practice statements below until you don't find it difficult no more. When you're confident, you'll be confident enough to tell them to someone else in real life.

This isn't a great moment as I am involved in something. Do we have the chance to meet at a later date?

I have other things to do right now, and I'm not able to make a commitment to this.

Please let me consider this for a while. I'll get back to you.

I would really love to do this, but_____.

I'm not an expert in this. I don't believe I'm the person to get assistance from. Instead, you can contact _____.

It's not possible for me to do this.

I'm not able to do this right now.

Sorry, we're not here today.

This won't work for me right now.

I'm overwhelmed with things to handle this moment.

Alternately, you can just declare"no. "No" is a full sentence. In the majority of cases it is not necessary to justify why you didn't say"no" in the beginning. Practice, practice, practice! Confidence can be built by practicing. Even if you don't attain the point at which it becomes a no-brainer for you, it's an opportunity to overcome.

Don't feel guilty.

Don't be ashamed even if you have to tell someone no. It can be difficult to assert yourself especially if you've always been a person-pleaser. The first time you don't say yes could be a traumatic experience. However, being confident and assertive is crucial to your overall health. If you're assertive, you are self-assured. You are promoting yourself.

This is where you'll also have to use the old habit of replacing negative thinking by positive thoughts. If, for instance, you find yourself thinking something such as, "I am a bad person because I didn't lend the friend I know money" you can say, "I deserve to be financially secure". Making loans to other people's money could cause financial problems and put your life in danger. It is therefore important to put your own financial situation first. If you don't have much excess cash, it's acceptable to not lend money to someone else.

Set up strong boundaries for yourself.

If you're looking to boost your self-confidence, you must to establish strong boundaries for yourself. Here's how you can establish your own personal boundaries:

Be aware of your feelings.

If you are self-conscious and self-esteem, you might be unable to recognize unacceptable behaviour. It is therefore important to observe your feelings about others' actions. If you're feeling unhappy and angry this means you're breaking your own personal limits. Resentment is usually a feeling that is felt when someone has taken the advantage. There is also a feeling of anger if you're not valued.

Establish your limits.

If you're looking to boost confidence in yourself, you must to define the things you'll be willing to accept as well as what won't take on. If you wish to live a happiness in your life, then you need to be able to resist being mistreated. Determine the actions you are willing to tolerate as well as the ones you won't tolerate, so that you are able to define the boundaries.

Communicate your boundaries.

It is essential how to convey your limits to others if you wish to build healthier and respectful relationships. Let people know the things you'll and will not allow. If you don't like the fact that your friend consistently late tell them about that. Get your friend's attention and explain your boundaries with respect. If you don't like the fact that the boss contacts you each week, tell him that you'd like that you not be interrupted during weekends. Be sure to do this in a polite and respectful manner.

Expect to be treated with respect.

Set boundaries and expect that people respect it. Make sure to call out those who violate the lines. Of course, be courteous. It will be difficult initially, particularly in the case of person-pleaser for a long period of time. You can simply walk away from those who are not respectful of your rules.

Reward for good behavior.

You can reinforce your boundaries by rewarding the people who adhere to your guidelines. Recognize and thank them for their kindness. This will motivate them them to keep being kind, compassionate, and compassionate.

Reward good behaviour.

Do you remember this golden rule? If you want people to be nice to you, you must to be nice to others too. Make sure you don't infringe on the boundaries of other people.

Be flexible.

You're able to break your limits in the event of a situation that requires it. As you gain confidence you will find it easier to be able to change your boundaries occasionally and then, when absolutely necessary.

Avoid harmful people and energy vampires.

Everybody has to face challenging people at some moment in their lives. Energy vampires and toxic people are those who abuse you, mock you, or constantly make you feel bad about yourself. If you wish to improve your self-esteem, it is best be wary of these people at all costs.

If you are unable to completely avoid them, because you are working with them or are members in your household, you can reduce the contact you have with them. Be strong for yourself. Communicate your boundaries. Be aware that it's acceptable to demand what you desire. It's fine to chase your desires. It's fine to not say yes.

Chapter 7: The Reasons Why Self-Esteem is Essential

Self-esteem is defined as an individual's belief in their worth and value. It is also related to the emotions people have about their worthiness or dignity. Self-esteem is crucial as it influences the choices and actions of people. Also, self-esteem can be a motivator and will make someone either more or less inclined to take good care of themselves and realize their potential. People who have high self-esteem are in a similar way motivated to take care of themselves and push themselves to meet their goals and ambitions. Self-esteem sufferers tend not to view themselves as deserving of positive results or as capable of reaching them , and consequently are more likely to slack on crucial things and are less resilient and persistent when it comes to overcoming obstacles. They might have similar goals as those who have higher self-esteem, however, they are less likely to achieve them.

Self-esteem is an extremely abstract concept. It can be difficult for people who don't have it yet to grasp the meaning behind having it. One method for those with low self-esteem to begin to appreciate what it's an experience to have a higher self-esteem is to look at the way they feel about the aspects of their lives that they love. For instance, some people are really into cars. Because cars are very essential to them, they are very careful with their vehicles. They make wise decisions about how to park their car as well as how often to repair it, and the best way to drive it. They can even decorate the car and show it off to people with satisfaction. Self-esteem is similar to that, minus knowing that, as a person you are loved and care about the things that interest you. If children believe that they are important and precious and valuable, they tend to take care of themselves. They make smart decisions about themselves and boost their worth rather than breaking it.

What is SELF-ESTEEM NOT?

There is much that needs to be discovered about self-esteem but at the very least we've been able to define self-esteem and what it is from other similar types of constructs. Learn more about the factors that distinguish self-esteem from other self-management characteristics and the various states.

Self-Concept vs. Self-Esteem

Self-esteem differs from self-concept. However, self-esteem could be an aspect of self-concept. Self-concept is the way we perceive ourselvesand our responses when we ask "Who is you?" It's about knowing your personal trends, thoughts about your preferences and habits as well as your hobbies, abilities and flaws.

The awareness of who we are is the concept we have of ourselves.

Self-Image vs. Self-Esteem

Another similar term that has an entirely different definition is self-image. It is like self-concept in that it's the way you perceive yourself. It is not grounded in reality, however it is founded on inaccurate and false perceptions of our self. Our self-image could be either near or far to reality. However, it's usually not in complete alignment with the reality of the world or how others view us.

Self-Worth vs. Self-Esteem

Self-esteem is a term that's identical to self-worth but with a minor distinction (although significant) Self-esteem is the way we think, feel and think about ourselves, whereas self-worth is the largest acceptance that we are valuable humans worthy of affection.

Self-Confidence vs. Self-Esteem

Self-esteem is not self-confidence. Self-confidence is based on trusting your capabilities and abilities to tackle the challenges, overcome problems and be involved in the world with success. As you may have seen in this report self-confidence is more based on external indicators of achievement and worth rather than internal indicators that are a part of self-esteem. There is a possibility that you have high confidence in yourself, particularly in a particular area or field, yet you're still lacking an enviable sense of self-worth or self-worth in general.

Self-Efficacy vs. Self-Esteem

Self-efficacy, like self-confidence is also related to self-esteem, however it's not a direct measure of it. Self-efficacy refers to the belief that you are able to complete specific tasks. It is possible to be extremely effective when playing basketball, but you may have poor self-efficacy is a problem when it comes to achievement in math. In contrast to self-esteem and self-efficacy, self-efficacy is more particular than universal and is determined by external success, rather than internal values.

Self-Compassion vs. Self-Esteem

Self-esteem, in turn, isn't self-compassion. Self-compassion is about our relationships towards ourselves. It's not about on how we view ourselves or the way we see ourselves. Being compassionate means being compassionate and accepting yourself, and not becoming harsh or uncritical of yourself. Self-compassion may lead to an improved sense of self-worth but it's not in its own way, self-esteem.

Factors that influence self-esteem

Self-esteem plays a significant role in your life , and it has an influence on the decisions you make. Self-esteem is the basis for what you think you are to be worthy and worthy of doing.

If you're self-conscious You are at a higher chance of not achieving your full potential. There are many factors that can impact your self-esteem. The four elements listed above can boost or diminish your self-esteem.

Your Childhood

Your childhood is among the primary elements that affect your self-esteem. As you grow older, your personality and your life develops, everyone around you can influence the person you are becoming, and this is true for your self-esteem as well. For instance, children who live in families that are unstable tend to be less confident in themselves and self-esteem. They frequently carry the burden for the rest of their lives.

The Media

Our obsession with all media, whether it's television, social media or printed advertisements is a major contributor to the huge self-esteem problems that plague our society. Social media's instant accessibility is especially harmful to children, who are under an ever-present pressure look and be portrayed as celebrities, public figures and friends.

Friends and Family

The people you interact with can have a major impact upon your self-esteem. Your friends can aid you improve your self-confidence, self-image and self-confidence but they could also abandon you. Unfortunately, there are some people in our lives who attempt to destroy confidence in ourselves by constructing our own self.

Family members can influence positively or negatively your self-esteem. A feeling of being inadequate with regard to taking care for your family members can result in low self-esteem. However, creating and working as a family can help boost self-esteem.

Workplace

A majority of time you spend working or studying. The surroundings can influence the entirety in your daily life including self-esteem. If you're stuck in a stressful and challenging job, you will often cause lower self-esteem. A positive and positive atmosphere could have a positive effect on self-esteem, and aid in building your self-esteem.

A variety of factors can impact your self-esteem. Each aspect of your life may affect you, but the individual with the greatest influence about your self-esteem is you. Begin to give yourself positive affirmations about yourself and stop fighting for improvement in your self-esteem.

Chapter 8: Practicing The Most Effective Method To Practice

It's time to take the most important test of my life. It's my test. I could fail. It's also an exam for you and that you might fail. This is the part you've been waiting for which you'd rather not be able to hear, but I'll give it to you in a straight manner. You're now required to practice your speech, and then you'll need to take a video recording of it. It's time to capture the speech on video. Like looking at my own voice, I like it terrible and extremely serious about it.

You are able to read all of my books and give me five stars or top-rated all that's useless if I'm not able to motivate people to write down their speech and practice them on video and again again. All I do with people , I sometimes work all day, every day, for five days for a client. The most important thing about my work is getting the clients to practice with video and then watch it on Sulu.

It is the only method to achieve significant improvement and continuous improvement. It isn't possible to do this through an image in a mirror, unless you've practiced in an mirror. And if you're just a normal human being with a nose that is crooked, I didn't want my hair to fall out of my. It's not your intention to give this speech. Your eyes are on your face. It's not the type of speech you actually speaking to others making your thoughts flow. It's absolutely essential to practice your speech on video. If you don't practice, you have a good likelihood that you will never improve. I'm sorry now, but you're losing your time reading this or any other book on public speaking when you don't record your own speech.

In the past 30 years, you might have had an excuse. Video cameras were rare very expensive. If you want a video camera, to grab your purse and reach for your phone.

It will record video in the absence of a tablet iPad, a webcam, or laptop. We're constantly surrounded by videos, and video cameras nowadays, so there's no reason not to.

The thing is, according to my estimate, less than 1 percent of people accomplish this. If you'd like to rise to the top one per cent of people who speak, all you need to do is one thing you can do: practice your speech using video. However, you must perform it in a specific manner because if you perform your speech using video but you don't examine it. It's not going to help you. It's a waste of time if you try to practice your speech using video, then go through it again and you think the voice. My voice is horrible. But at least I checked it once again, which is a complete wasted time. Actually, that's often more detrimental than simply wasting your time since it can reduce confidence in yourself. You feel like you're so miserable that you dislike your voice. You hate the sight of your eyes identical to mine or you were twitching around with a rings on your fingers just looking at what you want to do does nothing to help.

It's actually hurts to conduct this process in a systematic manner. Your presentation should be given to an individual from your family or someone else who has the camera. If it's just your hotel room, or in your bedroom, recording yourself , you're fine. You'll need to record yourself and if you'll have to view it. All you require is a clean piece of paper. Draw a line across the middle, and then write down every thing you like about it. Note everything that you don't love regarding any aspect of fashion or the substance. If you observe that you're doing this each three seconds it will be a bit of an strange anxious gesture. Take note of the fact that. If you think that my speaking voice is quite excellent. If I'm not running around. I enjoy my head moves. Give yourself praise. Everyone is doing something right and they'ren't making mistakes. Others make mistakes. You might not be saying they're arms. You deserve credit for this.

However, you should review the entire speech and note things that you like. and write down things you don't and then take a look and not be able to understand the speech back. The next time, it's an uncluttered sheet of paper. Take a look. Did you have fun with your nose less often? If you have made any progress at all. Note it down.So when you began and your negatives were that high, and the strengths were so high, you'd like to repeat the same thing again. The negatives go down while the strengths increase and you can repeat the process. When weaknesses come down, strengths go up. Repeat the process the number of times you can and let you know if you're satisfied with the results. This is the most effective way of improving your performance.

People said, well I'm not going to do this. Sam however let us ask this question. How often do you write an assistant or even just to record yourself and tell you to share it with of all of our crucial customers, send it to my teachers who will evaluate me, and then forward that to the center for media and all of our clients?

Everyone doesn't spell check the document, don't make edits or look it over and don't take any legal view of it. Investors simply release it in its entirety. What is the most frequent time you would do this? My guess is that you wouldn't do it often. You'd be terrified out of your head to write that out due to the fear that it could be a mess of errors. You don't simply dictate text and then send it to the recipient. You read it. You check it for spelling. You edit it and improve it, and you might get feedback from other writers. Once you've gone through three , five drafts, you'll be able to take a look and say , "This is perfect.

This is what I'm looking for. You're not anxious. You're aware that nothing will ever be awarded the Pulitzer Prize for Literature. However, you're confident that this particular document, whether it's a press release or a memo to a customer conveys what you're looking for in a clear , easy-to-understand manner with proper grammar and spelling. Then you hit the send button. You're not anxious at this moment since you've due diligence procedures to convert this rough draft that you wrote down into a final version of the document you're sending.

We are aware of that in the context of text messaging, however when it comes to spoken communication, a lot of us will say, "Here are the draft of the previous draft, and then simply because we're communicating to our audience, I'll tell that's not a good method of thinking since the initial draft of almost everything is it called is a rough draft, so when you're speaking to your intended audience and this is your first time giving this talk, you're giving your rough draft in front of the audience.

There's a reason it's so terrible. There's no wonder it's rough. We can't even expect it to be fantastic from the very first draft. What's the reason why we should think that the speech will be perfect? Let's look at what's actually happening. The majority of people, especially people working in larger corporations, that we view the speech as a complete PowerPoint presentation, or the text, so we could devote a significant amount of our time in writing, rewriting and writing the text for the speech or text, and bullet points in the PowerPoint it's an unnecessary wasted time. This helps you to get prepared to deliver a flawless presentation. It is a must if you plan to get your entire speech to be written, you must go over it and spell-check it in the event that you are giving it out to others who are using PowerPoint with text . I would not suggest using text in

PowerPoint however, if you are then you should definitely remove any typos and mistakes. However, for too many employees employed in too many organizations this becomes an obstacle.

You should be rehearsing the song now. We've had to finish these last adjustments to these PowerPoint and before you know it , the entire the week is over. It's 1 am , the speeches are at 8 am, and you're working on your PowerPoint slides. What's happening is that you've put off less important things, you've cut out things that are really important, like time to prepare. When you reach a certain point you'll have to decide that enough is enough on the PowerPoint or the script. Now, we need to practice. The best speakers know this. Ronald Reagan is a great communicator. He was also disciplined when it came to his speechwriting staff. He would now work with his team for months to prepare a huge speech such as that of the State of the Union address. He would then compel staff members to hand him the draft one week prior to the speech to be read. Then he would spend three hours every night practising and reading the speech during the residence in the White House. This wasn't intended to help him memorize the speech because he was using an Teleprompter. The purpose was to create a comfortable level an understanding of the words. but he'd then take a whole day to do a videotaped practice of the speech on the day before the speech repeatedly studying it and to figure out what works and as well as what doesn't. What about this pause here , about the thoughtful glance down there. It's not an accident it's not something that you're born with. It's acquired through the practice of hard work and it's achieved through a certain kind of practice. If you did not complete any of the assignments earlier , and you didn't manage to limit your message to five points and you don't have any stories, and you're left with only a monotonous data dump in which you can practice your talk over and over and again. It's going to be a monotonous data dump. If you do your practice with no video, you could making the same mistakes over and over repeatedly. As an example If I were teaching this entire course to you, but for the whole time I was doing this, I don't believe you really paid attention to anything else . considered that this guy was completely deceitful. He's discussing how to become at ease speaking. He's a bit uncomfortable in his body. And if I didn't even look at myself in video, how could I tell if I'm making that sound.. You can't tell what you're doing without watching yourself. The camera won't be able to love you. family and friends. They can tell you"hey, great speech. It's a good thing you're planning to. A good camera can accomplish this. The camera will show you exactly what you're doing This is the reason people are scared at times. They're scared of the truth, and they're unable to deal with the truth. Imagine how your audience is likely to be able to discern the truth. They often claim that they'll teach. I'm not one to look at myself. I am not a fan of seeing myself. It's true that you stare at yourself every day when you look in the mirror. Right.

What percentage of people are awake in the early morning? knowing that you have an important appointment to attend to the boss will be there and the board of directors and you simply rise and do not look at a mirror after shaving. Instead, you dress, put on your makeup and do not look in your reflection. I'm sure none of you have done this. If you're like the majority of people, every morning you glance at a bottle of beer. When you get out of the shower and look into the mirror, you shave or apply makeup and check your mirror. You put on your clothes and check your reflection. This means that by the time you leave your apartment or home before you head to your office or event to make a speech you're not concerned about food. Do I have jelly stains everywhere on my mouth? Or do I have a coffee stain on my shirt. Don't worry about it.

There's no need to think about it since you already know what you look. If you've walked into the mirror and you're aware of how you're looking today. You may wish you were more thin or differently but at least you're aware that you're appearing visually exactly how you'd like to be perceived. The most effective way to get across is based on your experience and the resources you've got because you've have looked at yourself in the mirror many times and it's the same with your speech, however mirrors don't aid in your speech. the only way to get a sense of what you're saying is to watch the video. There's no excuse to not do it.

I'm begging you. I'm asking you to help me. You've wasted much time, especially when you're sick. It's time to be playing an episode or two on Netflix or other entertainment instead of spending time with the public speaking voice. If you're not willing practise on video, that's the most crucial part of the process since you've had a lifetime's experiences watching speakers. You already are aware of what is boring. You know what you do not like. You're aware of the things that are distracting. When you look at the video of you and find yourself performing a tedious data dump or hopping between one leg and the next in order to grab a lectern, like you're scared to death , it's likely to be evident to you. It's also going inspire you to make changes to make improvements in your life. The other aspect it's going to accomplish when you do the things I've instructed you to practice on video until you take a look at the video and be able to say that you're an excellent speaker. Interesting. The person appears confident. If I could speak like the person, I'll become an expert in my field. If you work hard until you reach the point that something magical happens when you reach that point, it's impossible to be anxious about public speaking and be afraid to be filled with anxiety. The reason you're anxious if you're preparing for the stage or presenting is there's an element of you thinking that I could be boring. It's possible that I look dumb. They may not the meaning of all these things might actually be. It's not clear until you see the footage of you. Let me return to what I told you earlier using the analogy of the printed information. You're likely not worried or nervous about sending an email to your boss since you know that you will eliminate spelling mistakes. You get grammar errors. It's normal when colleagues have proofread it and you're not concerned about it. If someone asks you that you're at a relaxed dining out and they inquired about the way you have met your spouse or partner? It's probably not a big deal to not be anxious about because you've already said this many times before and you're at ease with it.

It's virtually impossible to become anxious when you are asked such a question when you already know the way you're presenting yourself. You know what you're going to say and how to present it. The same is true for presentations and speeches, even if you've not been speaking before to the live audience. If you practice the presentation on video and let people know that you're satisfied, it's likely to give you confidence. You've eliminated the majority of the issues that plague the majority of speakers today. I'd like to offer you a book and walk you through every tiny aspect. Do not play with your fingers. Eye people to get a complete thought. could go through the smallest of details but you're sure of exactly what you're doing and also what you enjoy and dislike. But you're not sure how to apply the same to your own speech until you've watched your speech on film. Instead of going endlessly on and on and on. I'd like to make more time to help you improve your speech. Check it out on video. Then repeat it and again repeatedly.

There are some who have trouble getting anything they like about their presentation. Therefore, you might consider bringing someone else to evaluate your presentation but always start by focusing on the good. Find out what they liked about. What was your experience? It's because I've seen this many occasions where people do 25 things correctly. But they did have other things. They would just be focused on the arms like it's the most awful thing ever and completely disregard the strengths of their team. It's not a good idea to do that.

Sometimes, it's beneficial to involve an outsider. Because they believe that they're doing the best job by simply explaining what's wrong. This isn't what's helping. In the case of a video critique, you'll need to devote the same amount of time. Strengths , what's working and what's best to improve on weaknesses and how to improve them. instead of constantly attempting to improve the strengths.

Before you head to the next lesson , please present your speech now you have already written the outline since you have five messages , and you will have a story to each of them or a perfect visual. Then, you can you can practice your speech using video. Continue to practice until you're comfortable with it.

Chapter 9: Believe You Can

The single most important factor that contributes to confidence in your own self-esteem is believing that you are capable of it, believing you are worthy of it, believing you'll be able to achieve it.

-Jerry Gillies - Jerry Gillies

Self-esteem is a reflection of how you perceive and feel about your self. This is the kind of thoughts and emotions one may experience - could be positive or negative or mixed about themselves. The more positive the emotions and thoughts are the more self-esteem you will be. On the other hand, the more negative your emotions and thoughts are the less confident you turn.

A feeling of self-confidence is crucial as it provides you an assurance that you are in control of your life. It can also make people feel content in the relationship. A positive self-image the person can create realistic expectations for themselves and set goals. Being self-conscious, contrary to what they say leads to a deformed perception of oneself, that can cause a loss of self-confidence and performance and depression.

In recent years self-esteem problems have become an extremely well-known and frequently cited psychological explanations for social and behavioral problems. Following the lead of the media and social commentators leaders, people are willing to acknowledge the fact that a low sense of self-worth is the root cause of nearly every personal and social ill including delinquency and drug addiction to business failures and poverty. The result is an enormous market for self-help books or educational courses.

People who suffer from low self-esteem are heavily dependent on their performance in the day. Positive experiences in the external world and positive feedback help them overcome the negative emotions they feel about themselves. These negative thoughts frequently affect those with low self-esteem. In certain situations, feelings of inadequateness afflict people who don't have confidence in themselves or about their abilities.

There are a variety of methods to increase self-esteem. In order to boost confidence, it could be beneficial to apply these self-improvement strategies and strategies:

Replying to the inner critic who constantly sends self-defeating self-defeating emails;

The self-care art as well as

Support and help from friends and family members that are near to your.

The most crucial step in boosting self-esteem is to tell your inner voice to stop. The voice in your head could be saying negative things about you. In this case, you need to affirm yourself. Replying to the internal voice that keeps accusing you of being a failure should be performed regularly. But, this is not enough to increase your confidence in yourself.

The next step is necessary to take on the path to having a positive self-esteem is to ensure that one must take care of his. The most crucial part of this is believing that you are a worthy person that is worthy.

It is not widely believed but the mental and emotional aspect of one's personality when combined, lead to self-improvement.

Our emotions can be a major factor in our reactions and actions even when we do not wish it to happen every now and then. People often view emotions as an indication of weakness, therefore people are conditioned to put their emotions to one side and focus on rational elements increasingly.

However rigorous and logical you be, you'll still be feeling. Someway or another some thing or another will come through to you.

A positive outlook on life is a aim to many who are concerned with self-improvement and health. Which is more important, the amount you earned throughout your life, or the moments you were giggling out of pure happiness?

People are prone to hide their positive emotions behind negative emotions. This is among the biggest issues that people face throughout their lives.

There is no way to ignore a bad event and attempt to make it positive ones. The world isn't designed this way.

As an example when you were in your early years If your goldfish died and you were devastated, you would feel very sad. Your parents might purchase a new goldfish, but the sadness is there.

The situation gets more complicated when you turn an adult. An argument with your partner the prior night will impact the entire day. You'll be exhausted, angry and your thoughts will be a blur. When you get to home after work, you'll not see the sun shining. You aren't likely to pull over at a market along the way to purchase fresh fruits and vegetables.

This is because the one thought that is negative has changed your perception of the reality around you.

In this moment, you'll find that finding a quiet space to unwind your mind can be a huge help to your mental and mental health.

The location is fairly accessible. It could be a real location or an imaginary one. It is best to completely immerse yourself in the experience.

Let's say that you have an issue in your head and it won't be able to go away. Bowl. Are you unsure of what to do? Give it a go.

You will be absorbed in the game. Your mind will break away from the thoughts of negativity that have dominated your thoughts for the last few several days or even hours, and you will begin making sense of a new type of information.

A safe place can be in many different shapes. It could be an album, a film or even an individual animal. The most important thing is to let yourself be completely engaged in this new endeavor.

There are still glimpses of the issue every now and then. Don't be distracted and become more involved in what you're doing.

If the bowling match or the music or the film ends, it will abruptly return to normal. It is likely that you will be tempted to go to your safe spot. Avoid it.

The safety zone exists as a support system but not to solve your problems in life, whether be large or small. It is only an escape way.

When you return from your safety zone feeling more energetic and at a higher level. You will feel happier about yourself and have more confidence. You'll see that any problem is solvable.

This is the way a brief escape from the harsh realities of life can improve your mental and emotional health. Make it a habit to do this frequently and you'll be getting closer to self-improvement.

Chapter 10: What is the reason women have a poor self-image?

Self-esteem is an essential aspect of being a person and is a key element in the ability of anyone to experience real joy. It allows us to feel valued from within, but at times even with a great determination, self-worth could be shattered by external factors. Women are particularly susceptible to this because the media and the society in general decide how we define "acceptable" specifically with regards to appearance as well as behavior and social roles.

Socialization and negative self-image

It's not difficult to see the fact that the general consensus considers "thinness" in terms of a determinant of beauty in the present day and the age of. While this perception might be shifting in recent years but I'd still say that this is the case to the majority of women. It is often believed to be inextricably linked with prosperity, the status of a person in society, and wealth. We see images of slim women across all kinds of media, including magazines and on billboards, TV films, and so on. Because of this constant bombardment of images, many women are enticed to believe that attaining this kind of look is the only way to get all they desire from their lives.

The mind's subconscious reverts back into the routine of comparison yourself with other people in this way. Family, friends and significant others contribute to the process. They may often and in a way, tell you not-so-positive things about how you appear. It is sometimes difficult to completely ignore them. Being constantly close to them, and being adamant about their opinions can make it easier to fall to negative thoughts if you aren't careful.

Another reason to mention is the hugely influential and lucrative market for weight reduction. Although some of these companies are genuinely concerned about our interests in mind, particularly those that are more nutritionally-based and health-focused companies. Others are just trying to sell false hopes of a better lifestyle by tracking calories or, even more dangerously than that, crash diets. They profit from our fears that eventually lead to us buying their products and attempting their diets that are not sustainable to attain our goals at a cost of $49!

They're relying on the notion that we're not enough and can help with weight loss. They believe that their products and programs will make us feel content and satisfied again. While it is recommended to exercise regularly and consume clean food to keep a healthy weight but it should be done in the pursuit of better health and not to gain approval from other people.

Body Image Awareness

The body image refers to the way we perceive our physical bodies. A disorganized body image can be an unreal perception of the body one has. The most common term is body dysmorphia and all of us suffer from this condition in some way. For the majority of women, it's easy to deal with using a bit of logic along with common sense. The ability to feel comfortable in your personal appearance also takes maturation.

Similar to self-esteem and self-esteem generally, a negative appearance can be the result of childhood experiences and can also be a cause of a poor perception of society later on in life. Naturally, family and friends can also be a factor. While you may be between the weight categories, deformed appearance can be a result of comments like "if you only lost those 5 pounds you'd look amazing". These seemingly good-faith and subtle tips can be a huge influence over time, especially if don't control your thoughts in a proper manner.

Being unable to feel at all attractive enough is a depressing feeling to carry. Therefore, the question could be. "Is there an option to not be in a constant state of resentment about your appearance? Is there a point that you will not be focusing on even the tiniest flaws?" Again, this is a part of aging however, if you want to address this by taking a proactive approach then here are the warning signs of a deformed or discolored body image that you should be aware of:

Being aware of your appearance when you are looking into mirrors

Obsessively comparing yourself with other people

* Always envious of the role models and famous people

Similar to issues that are self-esteem-related an image that is negative isn't something that can be fixed by simply sweeping it under the carpet. To allow a proper healing to happen it's essential to identify the issue in the first place. Recognize the negative emotions that you're struggling with. Discover ways to help your body feel more comfortable and free from thoughts that are irrational and that you aren't enough.

Dance therapy and movement are excellent alternatives to enhance one's body image. They can serve as a method to gain confidence and appreciation for your body by expressing it in a creative way and the exploration of. It may feel awkward and uncomfortable at first but I've witnessed numerous women blossom once some degree of proficiency is reached. It's a relaxing practice that has lots of confidence building and health-related advantages.

Low Self-Image and relationships

As I've mentioned the current standards of beauty are extremely challenging and overwhelming for anyone to reach. Everyone is different and must be encouraged to accept the different aspects of us. We often cannot avoid aspiring to these ideals. We want to achieve that perfect body or look, or even the actress or television presenter.

We are aware that it's the content of the inside that counts. Our bodies shouldn't need to be the determining factor of our worth. Nor should it have a significant impact on how we perceive our self-worth. But this can be an elusive concept for many, particularly those with negative self-images. In most cases they're already struggling with self-hate and a sense of inadequacy, and could be on the way to experiencing anxiety or developing an eating disorder the most extreme instances.

In this regard the negative self-image of a person can affect our relationships, regardless of type. It can affect our mood as well as how we relate to people at all levels. This can cause unnecessary tension on couples. In a romantic relationship the person who is self-defeating is likely to offer positive words to counter the negative thoughts in hopes of resolving the issue. But, even the best positive words and sincere praises may be ignored by those who have a negative self-image. This could cause further tensions and ultimately make the relationship to fail.

It also can affect the intimacy of a couple. A person who isn't happy with their appearance generally struggles with intimacy. Unattractiveness and low self-confidence can make them question their partner's feelings as well as feel a sense of attraction to them. They may be uncomfortable when touching or exposed in front of others.

If you believe that you're struggling with a poor self-image, and are noticing that it's already impacting your relationships as well as your life generally, you must think about having a makeover to your self-image. Here are some ways you can accomplish this, even if it's slow:

Make sure you see the achievements of your efforts

Focusing on your appearance constantly doesn't help you in any way. You're not the same as anyone or anyone else. If you continue to compare yourself to others There will always occasions when you're likely to fail. Instead of dwelling on all the flaws you have in your body, put your energy towards remembering what you're great at.

Say no to negative self-talk

Women can be very self-critical; yet it's not difficult for us to find our flaws whenever we look at ourselves in the mirror. We all recognize that there is no perfect person and we will have aspects that we would like to change concerning ourselves. But the capacity to be completely accepting of oneself is what sets happy people from those with negative self-images.

It's not going to be an instant change in direction. The change from negative thinking to positive thinking may be a long process therefore, you need to be gentle with yourself. Keep negative thoughts in check and work a bit every day, to create your self-image snowball little-by-little.

3.Take small steps if you're unhappy with your appearance to the point that shifting your thoughts doesn't work the list of feasible ways to achieve happiness will shrink. Try to be more patient and harder in accepting yourself fully or make a change to the things you hate concerning your physique by taking a small shift at a time.

Instead of joining the fitness center, dance class and the new diet program all in one place. Take each month off one at each month. Start with only 30 minutes of physical activity per day in the beginning, cycling, walking or swimming or cycling. You can then add a Pilates class twice a week in the month following. Once you've got these workouts in full swing, begin improving your diet by eating more nutritious carbohydrates and meals with less sugar. The process of tackling these issues each day will make them much easier to accomplish, and importantly, more viable over the long haul.

4.Open yourself to other people

This is the most difficult for some people, however, if you wish to change your perception of yourself from the negative light, you have to let the people who surround you know what you really feel. This is essential all the more so if you're in an intimate relationship. Your partner shouldn't be kept from knowing about your anxieties about your self-image. It's important to talk to them. By doing this, they'll be able to understand what's going on and also the motivations behind your behaviors and actions. The more they understand about your issues, the better they'll determine how to assist you in overcoming your issues.

At times, the love and support of family and friends may not be enough to help you off of your self-defeating image. In these instances it is better to speak to an expert counselor about your concerns. The advice of a professional will help you get more perspective on the situation, and guide you in managing the negative thoughts. They can assist you in understanding the causes of your self-esteem issues, and provide solutions that will greatly change how you view yourself.

These seemingly insignificant steps could be the necessary change to make a huge difference in getting your life back in the right direction. It is important to incorporate small adjustments into your lifestyle gradually with a method that isn't too overwhelming, but will aid in gaining a more positive attitude every day. Gaining a positive self-image is not a sprint, but one that you run. Just a small 1percent improvement every week will result in an enormous improvement in a short period of time.

Chapter 11: Looking The Part

Someone with a sense of worth can be confident and have a attractive appearance. Being confident and attractive is essential because it affects the people who surround us. It can give an increase in confidence and consequently boost your performance. When you achieve higher performance, it will cycle back and help us feel more confident. Being able to look at the parts is a crucial aspect of being confident and assertive, since it's quick and easy to master and yields great rewards.

The importance of appearance

According to the dictionary, appearance is defined as a show that appears on the outside or a visible aspect. Your confidence in yourself is heavily influenced by your thoughts and beliefs regarding your appearance. Your appearance is as important as it was ever. The first thing you notice upon meeting an individual for the first time in person is the appearance. This is why appearance is vital since you only have only one chance to make a first impression.

The importance of body language Language

The body language can be described as a type of non-verbal communication which involves expressive gestures, poses and physical signs that serve as signals to others. Humans are unable to perceive and send non-verbal signals using body language throughout the day.

A study from UCLA discovered that up to 90% of the effectiveness of communication is determined by non-verbal cues. Another study found that the effect of a performance could be determined seven percent through the language used and 38 percent by the voice quality and 55 percent through non-verbal communication. Your body language must be consistent with the words you use. If there is a conflict between your body language and your spoken language the body language is what governs. The body language components comprise:

Eye contact. The effectiveness of your message will be influenced by the level of eye contact that you have with the person you're talking. A person who is able to make eye contact with someone is generally seen as more friendly and confident.

Posture: Find standing and sitting postures that you can work with Avoid any rigid or slouching position.

Unrelated or excessive hands, face, and body movement A lot of movement could distract the attention away from your communication you are making. Your facial expressions must be consistent with your tone of voice. are making. For example, smile when you are saying "I love you" while frowning when you say "I am angry at you". A few gestures that support the message you are communicating are fine.

First Impressions First Impressions

It can take as little 7 seconds - - - and less than thirty seconds for someone to make an initial impression of your appearance. As you may have guessed, people form opinions about other people immediately based on their presentation. You don't get the chance to make a second impression. an impression. Here are some suggestions to help you create the right impression when you meet you meet someone.

Body language. Keep in mind that body language is up approximately 55% of communication.

Grooming and dress. It's not about budget but more focused on clean, well-pressed and event-appropriate clothes that is neatly groomed.

Handshake. Choose a medium-to-firm handshake grip. Avoid an unsteady handshake or too firm, which could cause discomfort to someone else.

Body Moving. Utilize a mirror or get the assistance of an individual to ensure that your actions aren't too active and are in line with the purpose the message.

Chapter 12: Finding Self-Confidence - What it will affect you

The next step is to discuss how important self-confidence is as well as what it can offer you. In the end, if you don't grasp the significance of self-confidence, then you're not likely to move in the proper direction. It is unlikely that you will be able to feel the effort to bring about this change.

This chapter will aid you in making the right choices and start the change your life demands. Keep in mind that these are the outcomes that you will get through the changes implemented.

Feel Happier

The first step is to feel at peace with yourself. It's a huge shift and one that many people do not have the ability to manage. There are some who will look back and be unhappy about their lives, and it has nothing to do with their own choices and has more about confidence in themselves.

If you don't develop the ability to accept and appreciate the person you are as a person, you're never likely to be content. No matter what you're dealing with within your own life. you're likely to not be as content as you ought to be.

As you grow more assertive, you're likely to feel more enthusiastic and more relaxed. These are the kinds of changes that are important because when your mental wellbeing improves, you're already on the right path to living a happy life.

Feel great in social settings

There are lots of people who do not appear confident in social situations and their experiences are extremely stressful. They do not wish to be noticed in these kinds of situations because it's likely make them look embarrassing themselves and that's never an ideal situation. Why should they face such problems when they can sit at home and unwind?

This is why it's crucial to boost your self-confidence and move toward a brighter future. As you begin to build the ideas included in this ebook and you'll be amazed at how social situations are less stressful to handle. It's impossible to get any better than this.

Social settings needn't be difficult tasks that are nearly impossible to navigate. Instead, you'll be able to tackle these issues in a matter of minutes. You'll be a completely new person in these situations and the people around you will be awestruck.

More Effective Results in both personal and professional life

Are you wondering why you're not climbing in the ranks of the company? There must be something stopping you from achieving your goals, isn't it? It must be something that isn't making it easy for you to impress your bosses, even if you're putting in the hard yards in, right?

Indeed, this is true because people who put in the effort aren't always capable of pushing forward. It is important to show yourself in a specific method to move forward to be able to achieve the results you've always wanted.

As you become more confident and secure and confident, you'll be in a position to impress your bosses quickly. They will be noticing your performance and results increasing. They're not treating you as an object They will treat you as an equal person as you merit.

All of this is by the picture you create of your talents. You must be confident. You are always at the forefront of their minds, and that's what matters the most. Be smarter and achieve the results you desire, not relying that someone will make an effort to endorse you.

Don't be afraid of criticism

There will have moments in your life when critics are not going to help you rest at night. Rememberthose instances where your boss ridicules your capability to complete the task?

What do you do at home when you're being ridiculed at home? It doesn't have to be ridiculed or even criticized for your actions can be hurtful.

If you're confident that you're in the right place, you're not likely to be noticing these issues anymore. They'll enter through one ear and out through in the other. This is the power of self-confidence. can do for you , and it is the thing that counts at the end of the day.

No More Fears

You'll benefit from not being concerned about issues that others might face regularly. This is not about fears such as spiders or heights however, they are things like having to make major decisions within your own life that could have a major impact.

You'll be able to make adjustments and make decisions immediately because you are confident in yourself. You won't hesitate, and if that's the situation, those in your vicinity are likely to be observing. They will admire your character regardless of the choices you make.

Will Not Seek Approval

There is no reason to be a person who is waiting around for approval. There are a lot of timid people who wander around looking in the direction of someone else to help push them forward to get them moving towards the correct direction but this isn't the best mentality to be in. Why would you want somebody to offer you that push to that direction?

It is important to believe in yourself, and that is the reason why you can enjoy an injection of confidence throughout your daily life. You will never seek approval from anyone else and that is a huge victory. You will continue living your life and laugh at anyone who attempts to put you down.

Naturally, one advantage of this is that you will be able to be open to criticisms that come your way with an open mind. You won't be weighed down by the fear of being criticised and will take the information provided in its entirety.

This is an enormous advantage that comes with being assertive, and shouldn't be ignored at all.

The advantages discussed in this chapter are likely to be a good incentive to you to take on the necessary changes be given to you. Keep in mind that the process isn't going to be simple however the outcomes at the end , and possibly over the course of the transformation will prove be rewarding.

People who have witnessed the changes in their self-confidence are beginning to notice the many positive effects they are able to observe in their lives. Do not be concerned about the challenges which will come up when you make the changes, because this is an integral element in the whole process. It is necessary to address these issues head-on However, the benefits are numerous when the change is implemented.

Tips to Increase Self Confidence

It's time to start working towards the meat. It is time to begin learning the things you need to know in order to change your mindset. It's okay to recognize the benefits of self-confidence but what do you need to do to boost this confidence of mind?

Let's review the steps you need to take to boost confidence in yourself and the changes that are needed. The advice provided in this article should be used both in the short-term as well as the long-term, to help you get started in the direction you want to be.

1. Zone Everyone Else Out

It is crucial to begin by shutting out everyone else around you. This is the main problem that a lot of people are facing in the present day. They're not able to comprehend the subtleties that come with listening constantly to the opinions of others. This isn't the best approach to take to the future.

You must learn to block people out. This will allow you to make the right choices. Do not worry about making mistakes, or dissatisfying others. It's normal and those who take their time will be able to forget about what people think about them.

The fact that you are zoning out everyone else doesn't mean you totally shut them out of your life. This is unforgiving and not likely to improve your social life at all. It is important to evaluate what they're saying and then repress it when they are just complaining. Sometimes, it's fine to be different and do what you'd like to do.

2.List Your Strengths

This may appear to be an overwhelming task. It may seem like something only someone on the bottom of the barrel might do but it really can be very beneficial and you'll be amazed by the amount of information you can put down as you begin to write.

The objective here is to list down the positive aspects of your life. This doesn't have to be just things that are considered to be 'important in your life. It can be that is as basic as the color of your bedding spread in your mattress. It could be as easy as this. It could be as simple as the 10 push ups you performed after waking.

Write down all these positives and then begin looking at ways to improve more and what you are most proud of about yourself. You are likely to discover that things aren't as bad as you thought initially. A lot of people focus on one thing they face in their lives and overlook the fact that there are many positive things that are often overlooked and ought to be.

3.Firm The Decisions First (Correct as You Go)

What does assertive mean? It's about being able to make choices and trusting yourself. When you think of making a decision but aren't sure, do it and go for it.

This isn't a reason to not investigate or know the basics however, if you feel that it's a wise choice make it so! This is the best choice to make.

What happens if there are obstacles as you take this step like you'd hoped? Do not worry about it, simply modify your plans as you make them. People who are assertive don't always produce perfect results, otherwise they would all be wealthy and live perfect lives. Everyone has mistakes and you must be aware of that too.

4. Personal Journals are Great

This is another tip that needs a bit of personal reflection. Do not just go through the data in your mind however, you should also be able to take it all down on paper. You'll be amazed at the clarity of your daily life becomes when you write it down before your eyes. It is more easy to sort through and any changes required are easily implemented. These are the small details that are most important in the final analysis.

This is a trick that will take time to become familiar with. Don't stress, begin your journal and observe as the changes occur by themselves since you're open to reflection on your own. There are many who do not have the ability to sit down and think, that causes them to be unengaged and insecure.

Your personal journal doesn't need to be an epic piece or run for pages. It could be a brief journal every day that will keep you motivated. It's just an additional boost to your life.

5.Don't Avoid Positivity

It is essential to not be averse to the positives there within your own life. It doesn't have to be a part of your personal life, but rather anything positive in your surroundings. Perhaps it's the child's smile. What can you do that will keep that smile for a longer time? Perhaps going out to get an ice cream treat and your children? This is just one of the examples of what you can make to make a positive cycle of happiness all around you.

If you're able to have this much positive energy in your life confidence in yourself that you gain is immense. Be sure to draw such a positive vibe, because it is truly life-changing and that's what people really want in the present day.

6. Don't Comparing to Others

Stop comparing yourself with others! This is something that most people do. It is painful to observe how their self-esteem deteriorates while others around them do things. It could be like buying a car you always dreamed of. Do not worry about what they're doing since they're simply living their lives the way you do.

Be sure you're focussed and looking straight ahead on your goals and life. This isn't a competition for who is more successful since, in the end the true satisfaction comes from becoming the person you want to be, and nothing else.

7. Understand What are your Dreams Are

The final tip of this section is knowing what you would like to achieve at the at the end your journey. Being confident and assertive is an ongoing process that will never end, you'll need to know what you're striving to achieve.

What are you hoping to see to be the outcome of this adventure? Who do you hope to be at the conclusion of this journey? This is the most effective way to ensure your success. If you don't follow this will go around in circles with no solution to be found.

The most enjoyable aspect of this method lies in the factthat you may be able to achieve something you've always wanted, but you aren't confident in yourself. What is the reason for this? It is due to the fact that you have never really sat down and thought about what you wanted, therefore you keep on going.

The advice discussed in this chapter must be followed with a steady focus on making changes. Do not just apply the advice at once and then wait for an instant change. This is one of the biggest mistakes that people make who are looking to become more assertive.

You must be aware that mistakes will occur, and that's a aspect of life. People who aren't aware of these subtleties won't be in a position to make their lives as they should. Do not be scared of failing as it's one of the main factors in reaching the stage of your life you desire.

Chapter 13: Life Goals

This chapter we'll explore how the topics we have covered so far in this book can assist you achieve your life goals. Everyone has ambitions for our lives, regardless of whether they're in the distant future or goals we're currently working towards. This chapter will help you understand the best way to achieve them!

How to Reach Life Goals By optimism

Positive thinking can benefit the quality of your life variety of ways, among which is to help you reach your goals. If you're positive as we've seen you are able to make positive changes throughout your life. The goals of life can be achieved through numerous tiny steps taken in the proper direction, and many positive outcomes are combined to ensure that a goal is attained. As you've learned, when you think of the possible outcome as promising, you will be capable of taking the necessary actions in order to make positive results happen. If you do this repeatedly eventually, you'll achieve your goals in life.

If, for instance, you're an athlete and you train each day to compete in your sport, preparing for competitions with confidence in your performance can significantly improve your mental outlook while you perform. If you do this you will increase odds of success, and ultimately, your results and this means you'll become stronger and more efficient each contest you participate in. In the future and with every one of your little successes taking you to the highest levels and you'll be able achieve your ultimate targets. If you started your training with a mindset of poor outcomes, which led you to fail and entered contests with the expectation of losing it is likely that you will witness these outcomes happen. In time, these outcomes could make you look further and further down the rankings in comparison with other athletes in similar sport, and the chances of achieving your most important athletic goals will be slimmer and smaller.

How to Reach Your Life Goals By Developing Self-Esteem, Self-Confidence and Self-

In this article we will explore how confidence and self-esteem influence your ability to meet your goals in life.

If you're able to maintain confidence in yourself that you have, you are able to face challenges and moments of demoralization with confidence. You can overcome negative experiences because you believe that you have done your best and this was only a temporary setback. You can fully believe that you can be successful the next time around. Being resilient is crucial in achieving your goals. Absolutely everyone is going to experience setbacks and moments where things get difficult and the ability to get through these challenges without becoming discouraged is vital to reach your goals for life you have set for yourself. You believe that you are an intelligent human being, and a person who is as worthy as everyone else and that is what makes your life more rewarding than people who does not see themselves in that in the same way.

If someone is not confident in themselves They may not see the reasons why they should be rewarded for being successful This can make them feel demotivated. The feelings of depression may hinder their performance on areas that are actions towards realizing their objectives. Some people decide to stop because they feel that it's too difficult and that they're not cut out to do it. They might feel that they lack the capacity to achieve the goals they've set for themselves or be hesitant to set goals in the first place due to fears of failing to reach them.

If someone has confidence in their self is likely to be to be comfortable seeking support and help from anyone they can find in the process of reaching their goals. This might come as a result of coaches who can assist with the mental aspect of their performance or even physiotherapists that help maintain their body in top condition, if this is an athletic goal. They believe that there's no shame in seeking assistance or making use of all the resources they have in order to solicit help to continue in their pursuit of objectives. They are also likely to be more comfortable in sharing their dreams and goals with others in conversation This motivates them, and will also show others that they are willing to anything they can offer in the form of assistance even if it's encouraging. If more people are aware about the goals that you're working towards, it doesn't just tells them they could assist you and support you, but also helps you stay motivated and accountable to achieve this goal as many people are aware of it than you do.

It doesn't mean that someone who is self-defying or lacking self-confidence is inherently less capable and less likely to reach their goals however it is the reality that people be more hesitant to talk about their goals, and avoid from seeking help to achieve their goals can make it difficult for them to achieve success. If no one other than the person who is in charge knows the goals they are striving to achieve. It is easier for them to pull from it or to abandon it. There is no one else to hold them accountable for their goals, which could make them feel as if they don't have any support. If they don't seek assistance, they're not doing all they can to reach their objectives. If they are pursuing music-related goals like, for instance one could get additional lessons, speaking with professional musicians or even visiting the music shop in their area to learn more about the most recent instruments. If they lack confidence that they will attain the goals they have set, then they could have a tendency to avoid all the actions that can assist them in achieving their goals which implies that they're creating to fulfill a self-fulfilling prophecy, standing behind their own achievement. Someone who isn't confident in themselves could also find themselves getting angry when a performance doesn't take the course they'd have liked that can cause them to lose motivation and takes the time they could have spent training if they were more resilient.

Goal Setting Techniques

When you are setting goals the method you use to define your goals will determine the success rate you will achieve. There are certain things to be aware of to make sure you set goals that process is as effective as you can. This article will discuss these points in this article to help you start setting your personal goals. Take a look at your new year's resolutions each year. If you are prone to stop working toward them after setting them, why do think that this is? If you set objectives in the most efficient method, you can ensure that this won't occur. It is possible to set goals at anytime You don't need to be pushed to make goals for the coming year and wait until the end of the year for new goals and you are able to set them anytime you want. Also, you don't need to make goals for the year ahead Humans are always evolving and growing, and the new year isn't the only opportunity to begin with a fresh start.

What Kind of Goal Set

The first step in set goals is to make sure that the goal you're creating will be difficult enough, yet not too difficult, and that you will be able to see the moment you've achieved your goal , and that it is something that you are determined to accomplish.

We will first take a look at ensuring that your goals are specific enough.

You must ensure that your goal is clear enough to let you know what you're striving to achieve. If your goal is general, you might not know when you've achieved your goal due to it not being sufficiently defined to be useful for you. If you have a clear goal, you'll be able to know constantly how far you've got since you know precisely what you want to achieve.

In the next step, we must ensure that the goal is capable of being measured or defined.

When setting your goal it is important to ensure that you have a method to measure it, so that if you are close but aren't quite able to get there, or if you do go over it, you can tell by the amount. If you are able to measure how far you fell short then you'll be able to determine how close you were in a quantitative way and will assist you set the next target.

You need to ensure your goal is feasible you're evaluating the goal you want to achieve like an amount of pounds to shed, you should ensure that you have in mind where you're starting. This will ensure that your goal can be achieved for you.

Your goal should be achievable

It is also important to make sure it's achievable not just for you. I am talking about it is humanly feasible. If you're trying to shed weight and you state that you wish to lose 100 pounds within one month, this isn't a realistic goal because it isn't sustainable or even feasible. It is important to make sure you're set to achieve your goals by making sure that it's an achievable target for you. If the goal is not realistic enough You will notice this very quickly after goal making, and probably give up on your goals completely.

Also, you must be realistic with the amount of goals you're making. Start with a couple so that you don't overburden yourself with multiple goals and you must carry on living your daily life as you strive towards your goals.

Your objective must be outlined on a timetable

You must ensure the goal you're aiming for is placed on the right track. If it isn't, you might be working towards that objective for the next twenty years, which could result in you not doing anything towards it in any way. Without a timeframe, you a reason to convince yourself that you're working towards it for a long time. The idea of having a timetable to achieve your goal will push you to the limit of giving you motivation and a sense of urgency while working towards it.

Note them down

When you set goals it is essential to ensure that you record your goals. This could be accomplished written on paper with a pen on the whiteboard in your kitchen, where you can view them, or on your smartphone on the notepad. It is important to note that you'll need an object to refer to so that you can remind yourself of the details of each goal. If you're overwhelmed, you could not remember your precise timeline or the precise number you're trying to get to. The act of writing down your goals will keep this in mind to ensure that instead of trying to guess, you'll be able to go back to where you recorded them and review every aspect of your goals.

The act of writing down your goals makes you accountable to reaching them or at the very least trying to achieve them. Writing them down gives them a sense of reality. If you have objectives you'd like to attain in your head but don't commit to them since it was "just some thoughts." If they're documented specifically and have an exact date it will make you feel that they are goals that you've set out to accomplish.

Another point I would like to mention is this: when you write your goals down, make sure that you keep them in a spot where you'll see them regularly. If you keep them in a journal you don't even look at will most likely make it difficult to keep track of whether there are goals you're striving towards. Placing them in a place that you can see every month, at least serves as a reminder of how you've set your goals and made them tangible by recording them.

Self-Talk

When it comes to setting goals Another important thing to remember is that you need to build your self-confidence conjunction with working on your goals. Although seeing your success in goals will help you gain greater confidence, you need to be confident enough to pursue the goals. Utilizing the strategies you've learned from this book to boost confidence in yourself and at the same time you work towards your goals you've set will significantly boost your odds of achievement.

Avoiding negative self-talk and getting rid of self-doubt thoughts, you can set yourself up for greater success in reaching your goals.

Self-Esteem Specific Goals

After you have read the book, you might want establish goals for your own personal goals that are specific to the areas that you'd like to improve on, which is what led you to read the book in the beginning. To create goals like this it is still necessary to follow the same steps as in this chapter. However, the goals will appear differently than ones that relate to income or weight loss. If your goals are tied to your inner accomplishments You will have to figure out ways to assess the external aspects of them. If, for instance, you're someone who claims to have a low self-esteem, and is then overcome by anxiety in the face of encountering new people because of this, how can you gauge the improvements that you're doing in a quantifiable and precise manner?

One method to accomplish this is to measure the amount of dates that you take for instance. The goal might look something like this:

Pick a date each week during the month ahead.

As you will see, this goal is very specific because it requires that you to go out to a specific date. This goal is assessed by the frequency of one date every week. This is attainable since it's quite feasible to achieve it in the beginning of the process of improving self-esteem. This is a realistic goal as nowadays, using dating applications, it's completely feasible, and the goal has a timeframe of one month.

If you didn't succeed in getting to your goal, due to the measurability of the goal you'll know precisely the dates on which you were unable to meet your goal. If you were short by just one day it is possible to set the similar goal for yourself the following month, and try again to reach it.

If you were short by three or two dates, it is possible to reset the goal however, reducing it to three dates within a month instead of. If you exceeded the goal due to the measurable nature of the goal you will know precisely the number of dates that you exceeded the goal. Moving forward you could set further ambitious goals for yourself since this goal was found to be easy to achieve. If you accomplish your goal could later set a second goal at the end of the month, which is like "go on five dates each every month over the course of two months" or something similar to this kind that is achievable and feasible for you depending on the progress you made in the initial month.

The reason is that, with a goal can be measured so precisely that you can alter according to how close you are towards achieving it at close to the period you have set.

Goal Setting Example

This article will provide an example of the process of setting goals so that you will have the idea on how you can achieve this by yourself.

Imagine yourself as someone who is frequently being asked by colleagues to join them out for a meal or drink with their colleagues after work. However, you refuse in fear that they won't like them or that they won't ever want to speak with you after they have gotten to get to know you. These fears stem from self-esteem issues. You've felt lonely and you have completed this book that is what has you wanting to take steps to improve your self-esteem.

The first thought that pops up to your mind is "I need to improve my self-confidence."

Although this is a nice idea to strive for however, it isn't measured or based on a timeline. We'll need to figure out a way to quantify this. One of the ways to measure this might be the following:

The number of new friendships that were formed

The number of times you go out for a drink after work

Amount of times that you have said yes instead of saying no to invitations from social gatherings

All of these are ways to gauge the level of improvement you have made in self-acceptance since as you've discovered from this guide, confidence in yourself can be closely dependent on self-acceptance. it is also connected to refusing to socialize chances or experiences because from fear of rejection. We'll choose the second option as an objective measure of self-acceptance growth "Number of times you go out for socializing in the evening after working." As you've figured out that they usually ask for you to go out with them on Fridays, after work you don't want to make your timetable too narrow. If they typically ask for you daily it is possible to create a timeline of only one or two weeks however since it's typically every week, it is best to extend your timeline by at least a month , or perhaps two. We now have a timeframe and the measurable factors. The next step is to figure out how many times we will accept the offer over the coming month. An ideal place to begin is to allow yourself at least one week of vacation in the event that something unexpected comes up that you're not able to be there on an evening on a Friday. Therefore, we'll declare that your goal should be to have a night out and meet with colleagues after work at least three times during the coming month. The goal is now measurable real, achievable, and real (as we examined the amount of times you're typically invited to social events in a month) It also is timed. If you had a goal such as this you'd record it somewhere and store it at the back of your mind.

If you're approached the next day and asked to go out with your colleagues to drinks after work, it is probably feel that same sense of anxiety and will want to not say yes. It will be the same for some time however, this time because you've set a goal and you are able to practice the skills you've learned in this book, such as controlling your thoughts by not letting your fear control you. You will be willing to say yes, despite your fears. After that, you'll be working towards your target. When you've been there for a few times and find that your coworkers are actually nice people that you have something in common You will probably be more hopeful about this kind of social interaction, but also other invitations you are given.

Chapter 14: Healthy vs. Low Self-Esteem?

Okay, now having an comprehension of what self-esteem actually is and what it looks as if you've got low self-esteem? What does it look like when you are confident in your self-esteem?

In this section I'll explain some of the issues you might be confronted with if you're struggling with self-esteem. I'm not sure this list of would be something you'd prefer to have regardless of the stage of your relationship or relationships you're in.

However, these are very commonplace things in our culture. In my opinion, the overwhelming majority of people suffer from low self-esteem.

Let's get started.

Clinginess or Neediness

It's possible to think of your self-esteem as the size of a bucket. If you're healthy in your self-esteem, it's similar to having an empty bucket of water (or most of the time, filled with water). Your self-esteem can be described as the bucket, and the water represents your personal opinion about you.

If you're suffering from low self-esteem, your bucket is leaking. an opening at the bottom. If your bucket is leaking from it then the water inside spills out.

If someone has low self-esteem, their opinion about themselves is continually dripping away. No matter how well they are at something or how many other people praise them, the "water" that is put into the bucket eventually spill out and run away.

This can lead people who have low self-esteem continuously seek validation from external sources. They are always looking for an "high" of being praised or achieving.

Don't get me wrong. Nothing is wrong with celebrating successes or receiving compliments. I'm sure that many people appreciate these things, and I'm not the only one.

However, people who have low self-esteem, rely on their whole identity with the results they receive from other people or from the environment around them.

Since their personal opinion of themselves is constantly drained away, they are constantly seeking to replenish their self-esteem by a world outside.

They may do certain things to draw the attention of others (positive as well as negative). They may dress provocatively or perform sexual acts in order to gain the approval of others and fill their bucket. They may seek out achievement or status (getting people to pledge to them, receiving the attention of certain individuals they think are more attractive or attractive, etc.).

It's all an attempt to obtain an external validation to fill their bucket.

However, since their bucket is brittle within it, they experience an unending drive to look for more proof.

The commitment of a person is not enough. It is essential for the partner to affirm their commitment to them.

The amount of affection is never enough. They need continual "hits" of praise to reinforce their confidence that they are beautiful.

The love of a person can never be enough. They require the continuous effort of their spouse to keep them afloat, emotionally or else they fall in a crash.

This creates a cycle of neediness, or other validation-seeking behavior.

It can also lead to conflicts in the relationship because one party always plays an role as "giver" while the other plays "taking" or "taker."

It's not just draining on"the "giver," who may get tired of continually assisting on"the "taker," but it can be stress-inducing on those who are the "taker," as well. It is the "taker" of this situation is in a vulnerable situation. In the role of someone who needs confirmation of"the "giver," there is constantly a lower-level fear in the event that "giver" is going to stop providing confirmation.

That means the only people willing to tolerate the needs of a "taker," in a relationship are the ones with the characteristics of "givers." Nobody else would be able accept the "taker's" incessant need for approval and stay with them long enough to maintain an ongoing connection with them.

It may sound nice and great, since, after all, don't you all wish to be with a person who is giving? This may sound appealing as well, and having a relationship with someone with the capacity to kindness and generosity is wonderful but that's not what I'm talking about when talking about "giving. "giver."

When I say "giver," I'm talking about people who are fond of taking care or playing in the position of martyr. This kind of "giver" is one who is so disengaged from themselves that they seldom take on any thing for themselves. If they do, it's often accompanied by a lot of anxiety that they're not able to fully enjoy the experience.

It will lead to lots of "Covert contract." We'll discuss Covert Contracts again, later however, you can consider them as giving to someone else with strings attached. That is that you are giving in the hope that somebody else will be reciprocated by. This can also lead to anger, hidden agendas, and other forms of giving with strings tied to it.

It's not fun.

You are blaming others or yourself

Another problem that can be found with low self-esteem is that there's plenty of blame happening.

The blame game can be blamed on others, and also the blame on yourself. The outcome could be either dependent on the personal preference for expressing their self-esteem issues.

Most often, the "givers," that we discussed a few minutes ago, feel guilty for not not giving enough, or even having to be "good enough." They're operating on "empty" and are left wondering what they can do to give.

Sometimes, the blame is shifted towards others, too after Covert Contracts enter the equation. When an "giver" or someone who offers with no strings attached, feel as if they've fulfilled their part to the deal, they may begin to feel resentment towards other people for not achieving the other side of the bargain.

This can be seen in small ways as well as in big ways.

There might be one instance of blame that causes an argument or conflict, but it can become a recurring issue over a lengthy period of time and result in a deep-seated bitterness towards a particular person (or group) of persons.

It is why people can end up believing they are "all people" as well as "all females" are the same in one in some way or another. The bitterness that is engendered can create an obstacle that prevents people from creating meaningful connections.

Self-esteem is a virtue for those who recognize that some people may attempt to exploit your strengths, but in the end you are the one responsible for the results you have achieved.

They are aware of this but not as a self-blaming or self-righteous attitude.

flagellating

In a kind of ("This is my fault, I'm unable to believe it's me") !"), however, it's more in a manner that accepts the blame.

The distinction between responsibility and blame is a matter of fact. Blame is a way of assigning judgement or blame while the concept of responsibility is simply to understand who is accountable for something or who is accountable for something. When you are responsible, there is no blame or "wrongness" there is no fault or wrongdoing.

It is possible that you allowed an unwelcome event to happen, but that does not mean you're an unfit person or anything similar to that.

When you are able to establish this kind of connection with your self (and with other people) this will help to improve your self-esteem on a healthier level.

Then, it's time to settle

We're told to never give up in our relationships. I believe this to be partially true. Certain people have standards that are far too high and completely out of touch with reality and others don't set standards adequate.

Concerning settling for settling use the 5x5 list I don't advise the client to make a settlement.

Conclusion

If you're reading this, you have realized that self-esteem is a nebulous concept and it can be difficult for those who do not already possess it to comprehend the way to have it. One method for those with low self-esteem to start to comprehend the things it is like to feel more self-esteem to think about the way they consider the things in their lives they are proud of. For example there are people who really enjoy automobiles. This is due to the fact that cars are very important to them. They tend to take care of their automobiles. They make good choices about where they park their vehicles, when the car is serviced and the way they use it. They could decorate their vehicle and present it to their loved ones with satisfaction. Self-esteem works in the same way, but that's not the case here you care, love about and is confident about yourself.

If kids feel that they are important and appreciated by their parents or their ward and family members, they tend to tend to take care of themselves. They'll end up making the right decisions regarding their future as well as about themselves and, usually increases their worth, instead of reducing it.

Self-esteem that is healthy and well-built is vital. We've observed that developing self-esteem takes skills, and those skills aren't any of them, and are still far from being achieved.

Self-esteem is a factor in how people identify their own values and strengths. They are not scared to reveal their flaws and be conscious of comments from others.

Instead, they'll be steadfast in their pursuit of their goals, and will be more prepared to take on the challenges and overcome them. They also can build stronger relationships with teachers, family members, as well as friends, and make the best use of their assistance.

The process of building and enhancing your self-esteem is a thrilling and enjoyable experience that has great rewards consequently, it should be considered seriously.

www.ingramcontent.com/pod-product-compliance
Lightning Source LLC
Chambersburg PA
CBHW071836080526
44589CB00012B/1011